T 25369

Teen Depression

Look for these and other books in the Lucent
Overview Series:

Teen Depression

by Lisa Wolff

TEEN ISSUES

LUCENT *Overview Series*

Library of Congress Cataloging-in-Publication Data

Wolff, Lisa, 1954–
    Teen depression / by Lisa Wolff.
        p.   cm. — (Lucent overview series. Teen issues)
    Includes bibliographical references and index.
    Summary: Discusses the nature, possible causes, special
problems, and both conventional and alternative treatments of
depression.
    ISBN 1-56006-519-2 (lib. bdg. : alk. paper)
    1. Depression in adolescence—Juvenile literature.   [1. Depres-
sion, Mental.]   I. Title.   II. Series.
RJ506.D4W65   1999
616.85'27'00835—dc21
                                      98-16379
                                          CIP
                                          AC

Copyright © 1999 by Lucent Books, Inc.
P.O. Box 289011, San Diego, CA 92198-9011
Printed in the U.S.A.

Contents

Introduction

EVERYONE FEELS DEPRESSED at times. Illness, the loss of a family member, the breakup of a relationship—these misfortunes and many more are natural causes of sadness and mourning. It is normal to feel depressed about a loss or failure. However, for many people, that feeling of despondency continues for months, years, or, if left untreated, even a lifetime. For such people, depression is a serious illness.

Depression is the most common psychological problem in the country, afflicting more than 17 million Americans and more than 100 million people worldwide each year. It is estimated to affect about 25 percent of women and 10 percent of men during their lives, and 5 percent of people during adolescence. It has been increasing in recent decades and appears to be starting earlier in life.

Since the numbers for young people are lower than those for adults, teen depression is often overlooked or misdiagnosed. Its symptoms often differ, too, so many depressed teens are dismissed as simply being "difficult" or "delinquent." Yet it is a serious problem, particularly when one considers the high rate of depression-related suicide among teenagers.

Because its symptoms are varied and often subtle, depression at any age can be hard to identify. Many people—particularly teens, who are undergoing so many changes that affect mood and behavior—are unaware that they are depressed. Even when they seek treatment, it is often for the physical symptoms, such as sleeplessness or fatigue, rather than the underlying cause.

The causes of depression can be just as varied and uncertain. In the past, it was widely believed that unexpressed feelings—particularly anger—were at the root of depression, and many psychiatrists still accept this theory. However, recent research points to an imbalance in the chemicals that regulate mood in the brain. Heredity, or the passing along of physical characteristics through generations, also appears to play a role, as mood disorders frequently run in families. Experts continue to disagree on whether genetic or environmental factors contribute more to the development of depression.

This controversy spills over into treatment. While traditional psychiatrists still favor psychoanalysis—the investigation of the unconscious mind through remembering the past—for depressed patients, a broad range of drugs that fight depression are now available. At the same time, many alternative therapies, including biofeedback, meditation, and the use of herbs, are being used to regulate mood, along with diet and exercise. Effective treatment may include any combination of these methods.

What is certain is that depression must be treated before it seriously disrupts the lives of the people it afflicts. Depressed teens often fail in school, become isolated from family and friends, and may fall into drug or alcohol abuse. Teenage boys may turn their depression into anger directed against society and get involved in dangerous or violent behavior. Teenage girls who suffer from depression may develop anorexia nervosa, a life-threatening eating disorder. And

Depression often goes undiagnosed in teens because some of the disorder's symptoms can be mistaken for the normal difficulties of adolescence.

suicide, often resulting from depression, is the cause of one-third of all adolescent deaths.

Depressed people of all ages tend to become socially isolated. This worsens their symptoms and makes it harder for them to get help. They tend to have small social networks and few people they can depend on for support. They often act in ways that keep other people at a distance.

The issues discussed in this book include the types of depression one can experience, how the illness is diagnosed, its possible causes, and the continuing controversy over treatment. Its particular effects on young people are examined, along with the treatments that seem to work best for teens. Intriguing new findings promise to shed new light on a disease that has kept so many teens living in the dark.

1

Defining Depression

DEPRESSION HAS PROBABLY been around as long as the human race. In classical Greece and medieval Europe it was termed "melancholia," one of the four fluids people were believed to have in their bodies that determined their personality traits. These unfortunate souls probably received no treatment and could be expected to remain "melancholic" for life.

Throughout literary history, writers have documented their depression in autobiographies, journals, fiction, and poetry. But it is only in recent years that depression has been understood as a serious—and treatable—disease. The biology of depression is just now being examined for the first time, and each year brings startling new findings. Researchers are discovering how subtle changes in brain chemistry can have profound effects on mood and behavior. Effective new treatments are being tested and approved for use.

An underdiagnosed and misdiagnosed disease

Still, depression may be the most underdiagnosed and misdiagnosed disease around. It is estimated that two-thirds of cases never receive a proper diagnosis. The form the disease takes varies from one individual to the next. Many depressed people lack energy and have trouble getting out of bed each day; others are full of nervous energy and suffer from sleepless nights. In teens, identifying depression can be harder still: While depressed adults tend to direct their angry feelings inward, depressed teens may lash out at family and friends. Instead of withdrawing, they

9

may draw attention to themselves through disruptive behavior, such as getting into fights or damaging property.

Indicators of depression

How, then, can we tell when someone is depressed? Since everyone goes through periods of sadness, it is important to examine the circumstances of those feelings and how long they last. Even intense grief triggered by a tragic event does not indicate depression as an illness unless it continues beyond the normal period for mourning. Another important indicator of depression is any unexplained change in mood and behavior. People's personalities change as they sink into a depression. Someone who was once outgoing may become withdrawn; a formerly calm person may become edgy. Unfortunately, in the case of teens, who are going through many types of changes, it is harder to tell when a change in behavior signals depression. Even those closest to them often fail to recognize the mood swings or personality changes as signs of depression. Sometimes more clues are needed.

To better understand the nature of depression, it helps to contrast the three most common types—depressive reaction, dysthymia, and major depression—as well as some other forms this puzzling disease can take.

Depressive reaction

Most, if not all, people experience depressive reaction at some point in their lives. This form of depression is usually minor and temporary, and the depressed feelings have a specific, immediate cause. The death of a family member or close friend is a logical, "normal" reason to feel sorrow. Many teens experience depressive reaction to moving to a new neighborhood or school, to their parents' divorce, or to the breakup of a relationship. The sadness may last until they have had time to come to terms with their loss and adapt to their new situation.

In some cases of depressive reaction, the sadness may be extreme. Intense grief is a natural response to the loss of a loved one. The key, then, is not the degree of feeling but how long it lasts and whether it is triggered by a particular event. Most symptoms disappear from two weeks to six months after the event, depending on the intensity of the loss.

In some cases, depressive reaction may be the side effect of a medication and will cease when the drug is discontinued. Drugs that occasionally cause depression include the anabolic steroids taken by many young men to build muscle. Depressive reaction can also be sparked by a hormonal change (such as just before a menstrual period) or a physical illness, such as a viral infection. Again, the depressed mood should lift when the body returns to its normal state. In general, intense sadness related to a loss should be treated if it continues beyond two months.

Simply knowing the cause of the depression may ease the burden. Counseling and family support can help teens get through a period of depressive reaction.

Unlike depressive reaction, other types of depression don't have a clear cause. Though certain events may deepen a depressed mood, the depression doesn't disappear when the situation gets better. It seems to have a life of its own. These disorders include dysthymia and major depression.

Dysthymia

Dysthymia, from the Greek for "abnormal or impaired" and "mood," is a mild but chronic form of depression. It is also the most common type, affecting about 5 percent of women and 2.5 percent of men at any given time. Symptoms usually start in adolescence or young adulthood.

The symptoms of dysthymia are less intense than those of depressive reaction, but they last for two years or more in adults and a year or more in teens. The depressed period is followed by about two months of relief, after which symptoms recur. One study shows the average time span is five-and-a-half years. Common dysthymia symptoms are disturbances in appetite and sleep, low energy level, and low self-esteem. In teens, poor performance at school, irritability, and conflicts with parents are often seen.

Current research suggests that dysthymia is caused by a malfunction of the brain's neurotransmitters, the chemicals that affect mood. However, environmental factors may also play a role in determining who becomes depressed. The disorder is common among children whose parents have major depression. Dysthymia is probably a milder form of that more serious disorder.

Because it is not a disabling disease, dysthymia is not always thought to require treatment. Many people don't recognize their depressed mood as a disease and instead accept it as part of their personality. Some notice only physical symptoms and treat them medically, without getting help for the underlying depression. However, people with this disorder often experience difficulty adjusting to life's ups and downs, tend to be in difficult relationships,

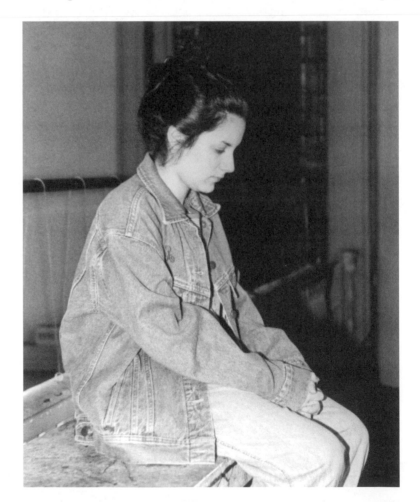

The symptoms of dysthymia, a mild but chronic form of depression, often begin in adolescence or young adulthood.

and may feel stuck in jobs they hate. Psychotherapy and antidepressants—drugs that act against depression—may help them live more satisfying lives.

Many people who are not treated for dysthymia go on to develop major depression. The longer the depression lasts, the harder it is to treat, so getting help early may prevent years of unhappiness.

Major depression

Major depression, also known as depressive illness or unipolar disorder, is a serious form of depression and the main focus of this book. Left untreated, it can lead to the inability to function and sometimes even to suicide, particularly in adolescents. Though more often diagnosed in adults, depressive illness can strike at any age.

The symptoms of major depression can be wide-ranging and are sometimes different for teens and adults. The most obvious sign is depressed mood, which is often accompanied by loss of interest in one's usual activities, fatigue, sleep problems, overeating or loss of appetite, difficulty concentrating, and feelings of helplessness. Feelings of worthlessness and guilt and thoughts of death are also common.

In teens, depressive illness often displays the same symptoms, but in some cases it may be signaled by angry, destructive behavior or sudden aggressiveness. Irritability and insatiability—the inability to be satisfied—are other common symptoms of teen depression. Since these are not symptoms commonly associated with depression, teenage depression may be mistaken for simple rebellion and often goes undiagnosed. Many depressed teens fall into drug or alcohol abuse in an attempt to escape from their feelings.

Many people with major depression have physical symptoms for which medical causes cannot be found. They often go for expensive tests that have negative results. These symptoms sometimes include upset stomach, constipation, headaches, backaches, and other types of pain. The physical discomfort often limits people's activity, making the depression worse.

The Symptoms of Clinical Depression

According to the American Psychiatric Association, clinical depression can be diagnosed when someone exhibits five or more of the following symptoms (not related to any medical condition or drugs) during a two-week period:

▶ a depressed mood most of the day, nearly every day

▶ markedly diminished interest or pleasure in most activity during the day, nearly every day

▶ significant weight loss or gain over a month (for instance, a change of more than 5 percent of body weight)

▶ significant change in sleep habits—sleeping far more or far less than usual

▶ extreme agitation or extreme slowness of movement nearly every day

▶ fatigue or loss of energy nearly every day

▶ feelings of worthlessness or excessive guilt every day

▶ diminished ability to concentrate, or indecisiveness nearly every day

▶ recurrent thoughts of death or suicide (or suicide attempts)

Major depression can also run in cycles. Following their first depressed episode, some people recover for a period of years, then lapse back into a depressed state. The periods of depression may come and go without being provoked by any particular events.

As with the milder dysthymia, major depression has been linked to a malfunction of the neurotransmitters in the brain. Research in this area continues to shed light on this once-mysterious disease. A recent study shows that the brains of people with major depression process glucose much faster than normal. This seems to be related to the sleep disorders that are common among people with the disease.

A genetic factor is strongly suggested: Teens with depressed parents are two to three times as likely as other teens to have major depression, and so may inherit a tendency toward the disease. However, environmental factors may play an important role as well, as major depression shows up in many teens who have suffered physical or sexual abuse.

It is hard to overestimate the importance of early treatment for major depression. The adolescent suicide rate in this country has increased over 200 percent in the last decade, and without effective treatment, many depressed teens grow up to become depressed adults. Treatment may include psychotherapy, individual and family counseling, and antidepressant drugs, and no single formula works for everyone. As an actor who has suffered from major depression describes it, "Each one of us is like a chemical electrical machine that's absolutely different from the other and is changing every moment we exist. . . . You have to shop around for the right doctor, the right medicines."[1]

Major depression responds well to treatment. The majority of people treated are able to recover completely.

Other forms of depression are less widespread. The most serious of these is bipolar disorder.

Bipolar disorder

More commonly known as manic depression or manic-depressive illness, bipolar disorder is a mood disorder in which a person has alternating episodes of depression and mania. The manic state may begin with a minor rise in mood—mild elation, optimism, and self-confidence—that escalates into overconfidence. At the peak of this stage, people experience feelings of grandeur, or of being superior to others. They may become delusional, believing, for example, that they have special powers or a special relationship with a celebrity, or even with God. In severe cases, they may become psychotic (experiencing a complete break with reality) and hallucinate or think they are being controlled by outside forces. For this reason, people with the disorder are sometimes mistaken for having other diseases involving loss of touch with the real world.

Source: National Alliance for Research on Schizophrenia and Depression, Myrna M. Weissman; Maurice Blackman, MB, FRCPC; *The Canadian Journal of CME.*

Facts About Mood Disorders in Children and Adolescents

▶ 7–14% of children will experience an episode of major depression before age 15

▶ 20–30% of adult bipolar patients report that their disorder began before the age of 20

▶ one-third of adolescents attending psychiatric clinics suffer from depression

▶ greater than 20% of adolescents in the general population suffer from emotional problems

▶ the onset of major depression is earlier in children of depressed parents (mean age of 12.7 years) compared with those of normal parents (mean age of 16.8 years)

People at the height of their manic stage are constantly excited and in motion; they talk feverishly, feel driven, and may experience an abnormal sex drive. In some cases, their energy level may rise to a point where they become irritable and easily enraged. The manic episodes are followed by a slide into depression, which in teens often takes the form of irritability.

Bipolar disorder typically begins in the late teens or early twenties, usually with a period of depression. Some people have a mild form, with moderate mood swings; those with the most severe form, rapid-cycling bipolar disorder, have sharp shifts in mood as many as four times a year. The depressed periods, sometimes lasting as long as nine months, are usually much longer than the manic phases.

Unlike other forms of depression, for which treatment with antidepressants is usually optional, bipolar disorder must be controlled with medication. Doctors generally prescribe lithium, a powerful chemical that helps regulate mood swings. Because the effective dosage varies with each individual and an overdose can be toxic, patients on lithium must be monitored very carefully. Antidepressants are often added during the depressive phase.

Teens with bipolar disorder present special problems. They tend to be less likely than adults to stick to a difficult drug regimen. They are often afraid that their peers will find out they are on medication and consider them strange or crazy. Determining the right dose of lithium can take time and patience, of which many teens are in short supply. Also, alcohol (which increases the risk that the drug will become toxic) must be avoided while taking lithium, and missing regular sleep can heighten the manic state of the disease. Staying up all night to study for exams and late-night partying can seriously interfere with treatment.

One teen with bipolar disorder admits to sometimes skipping his medication in order to be able to go drinking with friends, saying, "I like to feel that I'm independent and that I'm not sick, that I'm mentally independent."[2] Unfortunately, skipping doses of lithium can have devastating effects, since during the manic stage of the disease one can lose touch with reality. Some people, particularly males, become violent and destructive during mania.

Bipolar disorder is far less common than major depression or dysthymia, affecting only about 1 percent of the U.S. population. Unlike other forms of depression, which affect more than twice as many females as males, bipolar disorder seems to be evenly distributed between the sexes. The disease tends to run in families, and children born to two parents with bipolar disorder have about a 50 percent chance of inheriting it.

A woman who developed the disorder in her teens says,

> The hardest thing for my family was learning that manic depression can be hereditary. In my case the genetic predisposition comes from my mother's family, though it had not been recognized. My mother has felt a lot of pain and guilt, which I've tried to ease.[3]

Seasonal affective disorder

A type of depression that has been recognized only in recent years is seasonal affective disorder, appropriately known as SAD. It is also known as winter depression because of the time of year it strikes. Seasonal affective disorder is thought to affect about 6 percent of the U.S. population, with the greatest concentration in the north. A milder form may be experienced by as many as one-fifth of Americans.

People with seasonal affective disorder are particularly sensitive to lack of light. Research suggests that a gland in the brains of SAD sufferers is affected by the loss of natural light that occurs during the winter months. While most people with SAD start to feel depressed in the fall, some have symptoms as early as mid-August, when the amount of natural light begins to wane. January, the darkest month, is the hardest for such people.

Symptoms of SAD are similar to those seen in other forms of depression. People with the disorder tend to slow down, to cry easily, to have negative thoughts, and to feel that their problems are unsolvable. In extreme cases, they may have a "hibernation reaction" and go into social withdrawal until the season changes. Many are helped by light therapy. Some studies show that "light banking"—getting at least four hours of exposure each day for four days in a row—before the winter months can lessen symptoms during winter. The hormone melatonin also shows some promise for people with this disorder, as does one of the new crop of antidepressants, Zoloft.

Depression-related disorders

Other disorders include depression as a major factor. Premenstrual syndrome (PMS), which affects many women a week to ten days before their period begins, has only recently been recognized as a medical condition. Moodiness, irritability, anxiety, and depression are common symptoms, probably caused by a hormonal imbalance. Though most women with PMS don't develop symptoms until they are in their twenties, the disorder has also been recognized in teenage girls.

Addiction to drugs or alcohol is also strongly linked to depression, especially in teens. In fact, some of the brain chemistry found in alcohol and cocaine addiction appears to occur in depression and bipolar disorder. People often abuse these substances in an attempt to escape their depressed feelings. As one writer who has struggled with depression notes: "I tried every mood-altering substance to which I had access, anything to take me out of where I was, to make the feelings go away. I was looking for something that would make me normal."[4] When the "high" wears off, the depression worsens. Alcohol and many illegal drugs, such as marijuana and heroin, as well as numerous prescription and over-the-counter medications, are actually depressants. It is important to eliminate the abused substance to see whether depression is an underlying condition. Adolescents with mood disorders are about twice as likely to abuse drugs when they reach their twenties as teens without the illness.

Depressed teens sometimes turn to alcohol to escape their distress. While alcohol may offer temporary relief, depression actually worsens when the drunken "high" subsides.

Other depression-related illnesses are eating disorders, such as anorexia nervosa and bulimia. Anorexia, a disease

of excessive dieting to the point of self-starvation, usually occurs in adolescence or young adulthood, and about 90 percent of anorexics are female. Bulimia, which involves bingeing and purging, typically starts around age eighteen and is also seen mostly in girls and women. It was recently estimated that as many as one-fifth of young women in high school and college have at least temporary bulimic symptoms. The two disorders are related, and some women suffer from both at different times. Anorexics and bulimics usually have low self-esteem and often have a history of physical or sexual abuse. A common treatment combines psychotherapy with antidepressants.

Bringing depression out of the closet

As if depression weren't already hard to diagnose, many people—especially teens—do their best to hide it. They see depression as a weakness and think they should be able to conquer it on their own. When they fail in their battle, they feel helpless and ashamed.

It is important to understand that depression is a disease, just as real as heart disease or cancer. It has real, physical causes and can be treated medically. In the words of one expert, "Not treating a depression is like not having a broken leg fixed or not treating pneumonia."[5]

Depression is also a disease that does not discriminate. It cuts across all economic and social classes and affects people of all ages, from children to the elderly. Nor does it doom people to failure: Some of the world's greatest leaders have suffered from serious depression, including Abraham Lincoln and Winston Churchill. Churchill, who served as Great Britain's prime minister during and after World War II, described it as a "black dog" that tormented him throughout life.

In addition to all the medical advances that are bringing it out of the dark, many prominent people have been willing to talk openly about their experiences with depression in recent years. Author William Styron, winner of the Pulitzer Prize and the American Book Award, wrote a book about his struggle with depression. Journalist Mike Wallace has given interviews about his battle with the disease, noting, "It's good for a depressive to talk about it; it helps you. You bring it to the surface, and it gives you a kind of cleansing."[6] Other successful people who have spoken about their depression include cartoonist and playwright Jules Feiffer and Academy Award–winning actor Rod Steiger.

Among the many writers who suffered from serious depression was award-winning poet Sylvia Plath. Her journals, published after her death in 1963, are filled with vivid descriptions of her struggle with the disease. In one entry, Plath wrote: "I have been and am battling depression. It is as if my life were magically run by two electric currents: joyous positive and despairing negative—which ever is

Leaders Winston Churchill and Abraham Lincoln achieved greatness despite their constant battles with serious depression.

Journalist Mike Wallace has found that talking openly about his depression has helped him manage his illness.

running at the moment dominates my life, floods it. I am now flooded with despair, almost hysteria, as if I were smothering."[7] Unfortunately, Plath lived at a time when there was less understanding about the disease and fewer options for treatment. She committed suicide at the age of thirty.

Though it may be more difficult for young people to talk about their experience, they are dealing with depression at a time when diseases of the mind are being viewed in a new light. There is much more openness today than ever in the past about all types of illness, particularly diseases that affect mood and behavior. As the understanding of mood disorders increases, the shame once associated with them is disappearing.

2

The Debate over Causes

A DEBATE HAS been raging for years between people who believe that most behavior problems result from heredity and those who think these problems have environmental causes. This debate has spilled over into the area of treating illnesses of the mind such as depression.

Those who blame heredity for causing illness believe that the genes—the building blocks that determine our physical characteristics—we inherit from our parents also determine our personalities and the ways we think, feel, and act. Those who fault environment, on the other hand, believe that what happens to us early in life—especially the way we are treated by our parents and other adults—is a more important influence on our feelings and behavior.

It is difficult to prove either theory. The human mind cannot be examined as easily as a chemical in a test tube, although medical science is progressing to where we know a great deal about brain function. And more and more experts are taking a middle ground, viewing both factors as playing an important role in human development.

Complicating the debate is the fact that many experts have a personal stake in convincing others that their view is the correct one. For example, a lawyer defending someone who has committed a violent crime might try to convince a jury that the crime was due to a genetic defect—a problem the defendant inherited and is therefore out of his control. The lawyer will hire medical experts to testify that this is so. On the other hand, a student from an economically disadvantaged background might seek special treatment in college admissions, saying that her low SAT score is due to inferior schooling in a poor neighborhood.

Doctors who believe depression to be a genetic disorder are more likely to treat it medically, while those who credit environment will lean toward psychological counseling. As will be seen, strong arguments can be made for both sides.

Early arguments for heredity

Long before people knew what a gene was, they believed that personality was determined at birth. This belief can be traced back to the earliest Greek medical texts, from the fifth century B.C. Ancient Greek doctors developed a theory that four substances (called humors) in the body decided a person's typical mood. People born with too much of one of these humors, black bile, tended to be sad and to have a dark or hopeless view of life—what is today known as depression.

This view of human nature continued in the West throughout the ages to almost the present time. It wasn't seriously questioned until the late nineteenth century, when diseases of the mind began to be studied separately from those of the body.

Freud and Jung

The change in thinking was largely due to one man: the Austrian doctor Sigmund Freud. In Freud's view, personality was determined mostly by a person's experiences. He was convinced that what happens to someone as a child shapes his or her thoughts, feelings, and ways of dealing with the world throughout life. This became the view of most doctors for many years as Freud's school of thought formed the basis of modern psychiatry.

Freud's ideas, however, failed to convince everyone. One of the doctors who saw things differently was Carl Jung, a student of Freud who rebelled against his teaching. Jung believed that there were two main personality types:

introverted and extroverted. Since the same parents, treating each of their children in much the same way, often had children with both personality types, he believed that children were born with these traits.

Other researchers took this theory further in later years. A psychologist at Harvard, Jerome Kagan, did studies on three hundred infants, then followed them throughout their childhood to see whether the personalities they seemed to be born with changed. His research showed that the "isolated, quiet children were typically those who had been classified

Sigmund Freud, whose ideas formed the basis for modern psychiatry, believed that personality is largely determined by an individual's experiences.

as inhibited 5 or 6 years earlier."[8] Kagan concluded that about 15 percent of children are born inhibited, or shy, and that the majority of them would remain so as adults.

Some of the strongest evidence that certain traits are inherited comes from studies of twins. These studies show that between 33 and 70 percent of identical twins, who share the same genetic makeup, develop the same psychological disorders. In fraternal twins, who are biologically different, only 20 percent have the same illness.

Biological proof

In recent years, researchers have been able to prove with science that the ancient Greeks were on the right track. While there are not four humors in the body, there are millions of cells in the brain that play a role in how we think, feel, and act.

When Dr. Kagan's studies moved into biology, he noted that the inhibited children had higher levels of stress hormones and higher heart rates than the other children—even when asleep. This suggested that very shy children are biologically different from others, "in a constant state of arousal from infancy," he noted, adding "and remain in that state throughout childhood."[9]

To prove that children inherit these traits from their parents, Kagan studied their family histories. He found that an unusual number of the parents had mood disorders and that a large percentage of the mildly depressed parents had also been shy as children.

A connection between brain chemistry and depression

Certain disorders have been recognized for many years as having a strong genetic basis. The brothers, sisters, and children of people with depression have a 20 to 25 percent chance of developing the disease. Bipolar disorder can usually be traced back to some relative, though the disease can skip generations. It was long suspected that people inherited a chemical imbalance that caused these illnesses to develop.

The strongest proof that depression is biological came with the development of antidepressant drugs. Though this began as early as the 1950s, it took many years to prove how these chemicals worked in the brains of depressed patients. Certain chemicals have been identified that play a strong role in depression. Researchers have focused on two of them, serotonin and norepinephrine, that seem central in regulating mood. Depressed people appear to have a shortage of these chemicals. Antidepressant drugs help restore the normal balance of chemicals in the brains of depressed people. While scientists are still trying to understand exactly how they work, there is widespread agreement that these drugs have a powerful effect on mood.

Recent detailed pictures of the brain show that one portion is much smaller and less active in people with hereditary depression. The doctor who led a team of scientists in this study observes: "Most of the time we find differences in the brain that are very subtle. To see something stand out to this degree is remarkable."[10] This section of the brain had already been identified as playing an important role in controlling emotions. It now appears that it may trigger both deep depression and the mania of bipolar disorder. "This area of the brain may act as a set of brakes for emotional responses. When it does not function properly, abnormal swings in mood may occur."[11]

The discovery of the role chemicals in the brain play in depression has given new force to the biological argument. People inherit their genes, and these genes affect the way the body works. The latest research suggests that the way the body works influences the way the mind works. The question is whether this is the most important factor in determining who we are.

The arguments for environment

The thought that our personalities are determined at birth is a frightening one, so it is not surprising that many researchers reject it. It suggests that people can't change the way they think, feel, and act.

Sociologists—people who study the development of human societies—argue against these "deterministic" views.

They observe the changing relationships among people and groups to see how they are shaped by their environments. Just as Freud viewed early experiences with parents as shaping a child's personality, sociologists see the culture in which the child grows up as an important influence.

Margaret Mead: A voice against the genetic view

One of the most important people to argue against the genetic view was Margaret Mead. Mead was an anthropologist, someone who studies the origins and development of

Anthropologist Margaret Mead argued against the genetic view, asserting that one's environment plays a vital role in personality development.

humans in "primitive," or technologically undeveloped, societies. Mead focused much of her work on societies in the South Pacific to watch the ways social conventions affect how people behave. One of her major findings was that men and women act very differently from one culture to another. She discovered matriarchal societies, groups in which women hold more power than men and direct the way the society functions. This, she believed, showed that boys aren't born to be leaders or girls to be followers. They instead assume these roles in societies that encourage male dominance.

From her 1930s studies of primitive societies, Mead concluded that human nature changes according to people's surroundings. She found that people respond "accurately and contrastingly to contrasting cultural conditions."[12] In a society that depends on heavy physical labor, men will make up most of the workforce and hold most of the economic power. As technology takes over and ideas become more important than physical strength, women take on a more important role in the economy. These changes in roles, especially when they happen rapidly, may cause confusion. People who have trouble adapting to cultural change may develop symptoms of depression.

The strong role played by environment was boosted by many people's discomfort with the genetic view. If people's characteristics are determined by their genes, their fates would seem to be sealed at birth. Many people have used genetic arguments to take power away from groups they dislike—and sometimes even to condemn them to death.

Rejecting biological determinism

During the 1940s, there was a strong reaction against Jung's concept of inherited personality types. His views were adapted by the German Nazis to promote racism, which labeled certain groups inferior because of their genetic background. Hitler's scientists tried to prove that Jews were "contaminating" the gene pool of Europe, using their findings to justify the killing of millions of people.

Genetic arguments had also been used to promote the idea of inferiority in other groups, including African Americans. They gave colonial Americans an excuse to capture "inferior" Africans and import them into slavery. This view became increasingly unacceptable during the civil rights movement of the 1960s. As the idea of equality gained importance, sociologists worked to prove that differences among people were due to differences in culture, economics, and opportunities.

The high rate of drug addiction and violence in poor urban neighborhoods, it was now argued, was due to the hopelessness of feeling trapped in poverty. Lack of education and job opportunities and living in overcrowded conditions, not people's biological makeup, were the important factors. Teens living under these stressful conditions are likely to use antisocial behavior as a way of dealing with anger and depression.

Depression in a stressful environment

Many researchers point to the stresses of modern life as causing the recent increase in depression. For teens, the usual stresses of growing up, adapting to a changing body, and taking on new responsibilities are only part of the picture. The high rate of divorce puts an added strain on many teens growing up in single-parent homes. Some are forced into a parenting role while they are still trying to determine who they are.

A recent study observed children of divorced parents over a period of twenty-five years. It found that those who could not remember living with both parents had developed a higher rate of drug and alcohol addiction. Half of them showed serious drug and alcohol problems in their early teens. They also had problems with forming lasting relationships. As the researcher noted, "Divorce is a cumulative experience for the child. Its impact increases over time."[13]

The researcher also found that parents weren't discussing their divorce with their children and were shutting them out of decisions about custody and visitation. These children grew up feeling powerless about their lives and developed many symptoms of depression. A woman whose parents divorced when she was two years old and who rarely saw her father after the breakup developed early depression. She observes:

> I don't know if I would have suffered from depression without that early loss; perhaps my depression is wholly chemical. I do know that the only picture of me as a child which shows me laughing was taken before my father left.[14]

The research director of a hospital psychiatric department points to other environmental stresses that contribute to teen depression: "Education doesn't guarantee a job anymore. The security and supports are not there and everything is being cut back. All of these things affect everyone, but more acutely those who are getting to the stage in life where they have to make some major decisions."[15]

Peer pressure to have sex at an earlier age and to experiment with drugs are other contemporary environmental stresses. Without a strong family structure, teens are more dependent on the opinions of their friends, who are just as confused as they are about their place in the world. Teens are expected to grow up faster, with less guidance.

Teens growing up in a culture of violence and crime are at increased risk of depression, addiction, and related problems. Those who fight the temptation to join gangs, use drugs, or get involved in criminal activities may be ridiculed by their peers. They often become isolated and withdrawn in an environment that rewards negative behavior.

Another important factor that affects mood and behavior is a culture's sex roles. This gains importance as boys and girls enter adolescence and has been the subject of much debate among researchers with differing views about the causes of depression.

The high rate of depression among women

Certain diseases seem to run along gender lines. Heart disease, for example, strikes many more men than women until women reach their fifties, when the rates even out.

There is a clear explanation for many of these differences: In the case of heart disease, female hormones help protect women until they reach menopause.

Why depression affects more females than males is less easy to prove. As with the causes of depression in general, researchers are divided between those who favor environment and those who lean toward genetic factors.

Environmental and genetic factors

Women and girls tend to depend more on the opinions of others in building their sense of self. They are more likely than men and boys to keep feelings of anger and aggression inside and to try to please others. These traits are encouraged by a society in which women are the caregivers. Social conditioning appears to be a major factor in female depression. Most girls are taught at an early age to be modest and to hold back from asserting themselves. They learn to defer to boys in the classroom and in other social situations, and as a result they receive less attention. This often leads girls to develop low self-esteem, a major factor in depression.

Recent studies show that starting in adolescence, girls have a lower sense of their own competence, evaluate themselves more harshly, and set lower goals for themselves than do boys. They interpret things more negatively and rely more on the opinions of others in judging themselves.

Sexual abuse, which rises during adolescence, has also been traced to the root of many girls' depression. It brings about feelings of powerlessness, guilt, and low self-esteem.

These are environmental reasons for women to become depressed. However, some experts believe that female hormones play a major role. They point to the increase of depression in adolescent girls, as well as to the high levels of depression in women with premenstrual syndrome. The number of girls with depression goes way up at the start of menstruation. As with adults, the female-to-male ratio of depression in adolescence is two to one. Also, about 15 percent of women have symptoms of depression after childbirth, another time of strong hormonal change.

One theory why the rate of depression seems so much higher among women is that depression in men is less obvious. More men than women abuse alcohol or drugs, and their substance abuse often is not recognized as a symptom of depression. Since heredity and environment both play a role in addiction, an argument for either cause can be made here.

Men may also work harder to hide their depression. It goes against their image of masculine strength. As a journalist who suffered from major depression remembers, "I did not want people to know of my vulnerability. I was ashamed. It was a confession of weakness."[16] This denial starts early in life. The director of a psychiatric research department observes, "Boys deny they have any psychiatric or psychological problems; that's classic."[17]

It is likely that heredity and environment come together in making women more prone to experiencing depression.

As a result of social conditioning, girls often learn to defer to boys in the classroom and in other social situations. This, along with other factors, may foster low self-esteem, one of the factors in depression.

Children of parents with depression may have a genetic predisposition toward depressive disorders.

It is possible that as girls are encouraged to be more assertive, particularly with the recent rise in girls' sports, they will suffer less from this disease.

Finding a middle ground

Today, most researchers recognize that human nature is too complex to be explained by one theory. While some credit biology as having the upper hand and others continue to see environment as a more important factor, most recognize that both play a role in how people develop.

A child born to parents with mood disorders has a good chance of inheriting a tendency to be depressed. That same child has an even greater chance of developing depression if he or she grows up in a culture of drugs and violence. Educational and economic opportunities and strong role models may keep the same child from sinking into despair and self-destructive behavior.

In a recent experiment, scientists bred very aggressive monkeys, then gave the infant to a very passive, relaxed mother to raise. The baby grew up with a normal level of aggression—a balance between the traits of its biological parents and its adoptive parent. It even showed a normal balance of chemicals that relate to aggression, suggesting that environment can affect people's chemistry.

A new view among many researchers is that people are born with a certain set of tendencies. Babies show personalities even before they can speak and understand their parents' words. Some are quiet and tend to become shy children; others are noisy and active, and will probably be more outgoing. These tendencies are genetic.

However, socialization during childhood has a strong effect on the developing personality. The way parents, teachers, and peers relate to a child, and the way the child interacts with these people, can change the way the child responds to the world. A very shy child is unlikely to become a very outgoing one, but he or she can become more assertive with outside encouragement.

In this view, few children are born destined to become depressed, although children of depressed parents may be born with one strike against them. If parents, teachers, and others recognize this early enough, they may be able to help the child overcome this inherited disadvantage. Watching for early signs of depression may avoid years of struggle down the road.

3

Special Problems of Depression in Teens

T HE TEENAGE YEARS are a period of rapid and intense physical and emotional change. Even well-adjusted teens sometimes feel they are on an emotional roller coaster, happy and excited one minute, down the next. Because of this, it is often hard to know when a teenager has crossed the line from normal feelings of adolescent turmoil to depression.

As a woman who suffered from depression as a teen notes,

> As a teenager I was moody and self-absorbed. Of course, that's common for teenagers, so my behavior was written off as normal. Unfortunately, I also had no interest in school, sports, clubs, etc. Part of it was the fog that was beginning to descend over my mind from time to time and part of it was the fear of failing in anything new.[18]

While official estimates show that 5 percent of teens suffer from depression, that figure is probably low. Some recent studies report that more than 20 percent of adolescents have emotional problems and that one-third of those being treated in psychiatric clinics are depressed.

Problems with diagnosing teen depression

Adolescent depression is particularly hard to diagnose, and teens—who more than any other age group want to "fit in"—work especially hard at hiding their feelings. If they are failing in school, they may act as though they don't care and go out drinking with friends instead of studying, when in fact they are worrying about how they are falling further and further behind. While an adult might react to a failed relationship by turning inward, a teenager might instead turn to drugs and violence.

These outer-directed behaviors—lashing out at parents and other authority figures, destroying property, and acting in other antisocial ways—often mask teen depression. Because they are interpreted as signs of anger and rebellion, people often miss the feelings of hopelessness they hide.

Other teens sometimes show their depression symbolically, such as by wearing black clothes or writing poetry about death. These signs also tend to be dismissed as normal acts of teenage rebellion.

There is usually a great deal of anger involved in teen depression. Adolescents are often told that their teenage years are supposed to be the happiest time of their lives. Some teens may feel they are letting their parents down with their unhappiness and that they have no right to feel the way they do. They are often ashamed by their negative behavior, which makes them feel worse about themselves and even more depressed.

Instead of showing the more typical symptoms, such as sadness and withdrawal, teens often express their depression through angry, destructive acts. They may channel their feelings into antisocial, often violent, behavior.

Antisocial behavior

Antisocial behavior can be defined as any behavior that aims to offend a society. It can include anything from disobeying nuisance laws, such as smoking in a place where it is forbidden, to relatively minor acts of vandalism, such as spray painting graffiti on public property, to serious acts of violence. Its goal is usually to demand attention by violating social norms.

Most teens sometimes act in ways designed to draw negative attention from adults. They may dye their hair purple, pierce their eyebrows or lips, or wear clothing resembling those of street gangs. In most cases, the behavior is fairly

While rebellion in adolescence is a normal part of development, drastic changes in appearance may suggest emotional problems.

innocent. It may shock or anger parents or teachers, but it doesn't cause any real harm. It is when the behavior becomes more extreme that it climbs from common teen rebellion to social deviance.

Serious antisocial behavior is often a sign of depression and a cry for help. However, because of its destructive nature, it frequently has the opposite effect. Unless they understand that a rebellious teen is in pain, adults will often react with anger or disgust and turn away instead of listening. This type of reaction further alienates the teen and may trigger more destructive behavior.

Teens who strike out at the world instead of dealing with their emotions often feel that any activity—even if dangerous or destructive—is better than facing their problems. Their antisocial behavior causes them to feel guilt, which makes their depression worse. Some teens feel so guilty about their acts that they may unconsciously set themselves up to get caught and punished.

Teens who act out their feelings through aggression often reflect aggressive behavior in the home. They may be copying the behavior of an abusive parent. A recent nationwide survey of teens shows that nearly 43 percent believe violent behavior is learned from parents. Other studies show that children who witness violence in the home are likely to become depressed and to act out their depression aggressively.

Teen violence

The ways in which teens are lashing out at society are becoming more violent and dangerous. A recent Department of Justice study predicts that one in five Americans will have committed a violent crime by the age of eighteen. Angry teens often act without considering the consequences of their actions. With guns so widely available in the United States, this often leads to serious injury and even death.

Antisocial behavior usually begins with minor acts of defiance and builds toward more serious aggression if not treated early. Teens who turn their depressed feelings into aggressive behavior often become a danger to society and to themselves.

Some teens who behave aggressively join street gangs. In rejecting their families and society, they find a substitute family and a new, antisocial set of rules by which to live. They often feel pressured to join these gangs, particularly if they lack a strong support system at home. Depressed teens who feel misunderstood and distrust adults fall in easily with those who promise to accept and protect them.

Aggressive or violent behavior is much more common among teenage boys than among girls, who tend to turn their anger against themselves. However, some teenage girls find ways of behaving that draw negative attention from society. They may shoplift or steal money from their parents, or they may act out by getting into inappropriate sexual relationships. Girls with low self-esteem often equate sex with love, feeling that if they can't be loved for themselves, at least they can be loved physically.

Teens who behave in antisocial ways need treatment for the underlying causes of their actions. Without help, they may end up in dangerous situations that lead to jail and to ruined lives. This danger is often compounded by the abuse of alcohol or drugs.

Alcohol abuse

Drinking has been part of American culture since the first European settlers reached the shores of New England. Americans drink alcohol to socialize and to celebrate, to relax and to forget their troubles. Two-thirds of the adult population consume some quantity of alcohol. It is no wonder, then, that so many teens experiment with this legal drug.

Alcohol is often glamorized in Western culture. From the whiskey-drinking cowboy to James Bond's dry martinis, movies and literature make drinking look masculine and sophisticated. Teens who are trying to look more adult often think drinking will make them seem mature and more appealing to the opposite sex. The real picture drunkenness and alcoholism presents, however, is very different from this image. And while many teens will grow up to drink responsibly, others will become a danger to themselves and to society.

Teens often use alcohol to escape from anxiety and depression. It can temporarily lift one's mood and numb unpleasant feelings. A teen might drink to ease the nervousness of a first date or to forget about a fight with a parent. Many teenagers drink to be "part of the gang," to fit in with their drinking peers. They may be pressured into drinking by friends who are heavy drinkers.

The physical effects of drinking range from mild changes in mood to loss of coordination, vision, balance, and speech. Since different people tolerate varying amounts, it is hard to measure how much alcohol it takes for someone to be considered drunk. Small women tend to reach this stage quickly, presenting a particular problem for teenage girls. Drinking is usually involved in date rape, as girls who have been drinking are in a poor position to show lack of consent.

In extreme cases, heavy alcohol consumption can damage brain function, cause the drinker to lose consciousness, and even kill. Long-term effects of heavy drinking include liver damage, and one in five heavy drinkers ends up with liver disease.

Teens often use alcohol to ease their anxiety and to cope with the difficulties of adolescence.

Teen alcoholism

Not all teens who drink will have problems with alcohol, but some will become alcoholics. Alcohol is a highly addictive drug, and many people are predisposed to alcohol addiction. Children of alcoholics are four to five times as likely to develop the disease as are other people, and at least half of all people treated for alcoholism have a family history of the disease. There appears to be a strong hereditary factor in alcohol addiction.

Many scientists now believe that children of alcoholics inherit differences in the brain's ability to process alcohol. Alcoholics have an imbalance in the brain's receptor for a neurotransmitter that regulates anxiety. Drinking has been shown to raise the level of this chemical to normal. However, environment also seems to play a role in triggering or worsening the tendency to become addicted to alcohol.

Depressed teens are especially likely to have problems with alcohol. Although they drink to lift their dark mood, alcohol is in fact a depressant. After the initial high, it slows down brain activity. The person will then commonly drink more to regain the high, only to sink further into depression when it is over. It is difficult to treat other problems when one is caught up in alcohol addiction, and alcoholics almost always deny their dependence on drinking.

Alcohol can seriously complicate other disorders. It is particularly dangerous when used by people with bipolar disorder. One man recalls how alcoholism complicated his manic depression:

> During those years I was in complete denial of what alcohol was doing to the chemical makeup of my body. I drank in order to suppress the feeling of mania and depression. The more I drank the sicker I became, yet I would not address my alcohol problem because alcohol had become my best friend. Denial runs deep! [19]

Alcohol abuse is a serious problem that goes way beyond the individual drinker. Many thousands of deaths in the United States each year result from the abuse of alcohol. It is a factor in half of all homicides, suicides, and traffic accidents in the country. Alcohol also plays a major role in many other crimes, including domestic violence and child abuse.

Treatment and support

Treatment for alcohol abuse often combines medical care with counseling. Addicted teens may need to enter a hospital program, where their withdrawal from alcohol can be monitored. These programs usually include counseling once the recovering teen is well enough to participate in individual or group therapy.

Programs such as Alcoholics Anonymous offer group support in staying sober. Some of their meetings are exclusively for young people, giving teens the support of their peers.

Drug abuse

Like alcohol, drugs are a popular escape for depressed teens. And as with drinking, drug use often leads to addiction. Any continuous, compulsive use is considered addiction.

Teen drug abuse in the United States has increased sharply since 1992, along with drug-related visits to hospital emergency rooms. Between 1992 and 1995, the increase in drug abuse among twelve- to seventeen-year-olds was 78 percent. No increase among adults was reported during this period.

Many teens experiment with drugs for the same reasons they try alcohol: to go along with their peers, to appear mature or sophisticated, as a form of rebellion, or to try to boost their mood or calm their nerves. They seldom worry about becoming addicted because, as with so many things, they believe they are immune to addiction.

Drug addiction is a complex issue because it is so wide-ranging. It is by no means limited to illegal drugs such as cocaine or heroin. Between 2 and 3 million Americans are

Recovering addicts attend an alcohol treatment program. Groups such as Alcoholics Anonymous offer ongoing support in remaining sober.

addicted to prescription medicines, and many are dependent on over-the-counter medications like diet pills, which are often abused by teenage girls. However, the drugs teens are most likely to abuse are those they use recreationally, which are usually illegal.

Frequently abused drugs

Drugs have a wide variety of effects on the body and mind. Some, including sleeping pills and drugs that fight anxiety, depress the central nervous system. These are among the most widely prescribed drugs in the United States, with about 7 million people taking them at least once a week. They are usually prescribed for a limited period of time to treat a temporary problem, but people grow dependent on them and find ways to continue their supply.

Other drugs, many of which are illegal, act as stimulants. These include amphetamines, or "uppers," cocaine, and its smoked form, crack. They are highly addictive and tend to cause rapid speech, nervousness, and wide swings between high and low moods. Many people who become addicted to amphetamines try to calm their nerves with de-

Teens who use marijuana may be unaware of the serious medical problems associated with chronic use.

pressants, or "downers," and get caught in a vicious cycle with both types of drugs. Cocaine use is a particularly serious problem, with an estimated 2 million cocaine addicts in the country. The increase in cocaine use among teens from 1992 to 1995 was 166 percent.

Opiates are another form of highly addictive drug that are frequently abused. This category includes opium, morphine, and heroin. Opiate addiction commonly causes depression, anxiety, and low self-esteem, so even a previously healthy teen who uses any of these drugs can wind up depressed. Emergency-room treatment of teens for heroin use went up 58 percent between 1992 and 1995.

Cannabis (most commonly used as marijuana) depresses short-term memory, motivation, and energy levels. Teens who are wary of "hard" drugs often think smoking marijuana is risk-free because it is not highly addictive. However, continued use can cause serious medical problems, such as increased heart rate, vision problems, changes in sex hormones, and lung problems, including an increased risk of lung cancer. Marijuana use among teens rose by 37 percent from 1992 to 1995, and since 1982, emergency-room visits due to problems from marijuana went up 96 percent. Many marijuana users go on to use cocaine.

Teens who use drugs tend to have weak family support and to be easily swayed by their peers. As with alcoholism, there may be a genetic tendency toward drug addiction, though it is more common in teens living in poverty and those with troubled family histories. Families who are embarrassed by their children's drug use may help already secretive teens hide the problem by denying it. This makes seeking treatment even more difficult.

Breaking drug dependence

Dependence on drugs is hard to break. As with alcohol, the body becomes more and more able to handle larger doses as use is increased. The body must be cleansed of these large amounts of drugs before withdrawal and recovery can begin. Many people continue to use drugs because they fear the pain of withdrawal, which can take from days to weeks depending on the individual. Withdrawal from drugs is dangerous without professional supervision.

No single form of treatment seems to work for everyone. Treatments include self-help groups such as Narcotics Anonymous, residential treatment programs, psychotherapy, and outpatient maintenance programs. Group treatment seems to work best with teens, and since the problem almost always involves the family, treatment is usually most effective if family members are involved.

The problems of teen drug abuse are far-reaching. Teens who are caught possessing or using illegal drugs are subject to prosecution, which may include a jail sentence. They establish criminal records that may haunt them the rest of their lives. And many, particularly males, go on to commit more serious crimes to support an increasingly expensive drug habit. The total cost to the individual, the family, and society can be devastating.

Eating disorders

A very large number of young women today have obsessions with food and dieting. A recent study shows that half of nine-year-old girls and 80 percent of those ten and eleven years old are already dieting, though few are overweight. This unrealistic perception girls tend to have of themselves often leads to serious eating disorders.

Eating disorders affect millions of American women and commonly begin in adolescence. Adolescent girls often have low self-esteem and very mixed feelings about their changing bodies and emotions. They are also especially likely to be affected by glamorous images in the media of very thin women and by slick magazines with cover stories about losing weight. Food and dieting become distractions from the difficult issues of growing up and, for many girls, the focus of an illness.

Anorexia nervosa

Anorexia nervosa is probably the only disorder of the mind found almost exclusively among teens. It is an eating disorder that usually occurs during adolescence, and about 90 percent of anorexics are female. The disease is estimated to affect 1 percent of girls and women.

Anorexia means lack of appetite, but anorexics are in fact obsessed with food. They think about it constantly and often cook for others at the same time they are starving themselves. Anorexics have an unrealistic dread of becoming fat, even when they have dieted themselves to skeletal thinness.

While food and dieting seem to be central issues in this disorder, beneath them lie low self-esteem and depression. The starvation is an anorexic's way of trying to gain control of her life by controlling her appetite and body. It is also an attempt to avoid sexual maturity. After losing a certain percentage of her weight, an anorexic girl will stop menstruating and look less like a woman.

Although some of the traits of anorexia nervosa may be inherited, most researchers believe that environmental factors play a bigger role. Anorexics tend to come from families with high standards of achievement. Like their parents, they are often perfectionists, and they feel hopeless when

Adolescent girls, who are often influenced by the media's glamorous portrayal of thin women, sometimes find it difficult to live up to such standards and may develop harmful preoccupations with food and dieting.

they can't meet impossible goals. Their poor self-image also makes them vulnerable to cultural messages that glorify thinness, such as ads featuring abnormally thin models. Many young women who enter professions that demand thinness, such as dancing or modeling, become anorexic.

The clearest warning sign of anorexia is rapid weight loss and extreme thinness. Other indicators include excessive dieting and exercising, a distorted body image (mistakenly seeing oneself as fat), abnormal preoccupation with food, an increase in facial or body hair due to hormonal imbalance, and insomnia. Anorexics almost always deny these symptoms and become angry and defensive when confronted with their behavior.

Anorexia nervosa is a very serious disease. Nearly 15 percent of anorexics die of its complications, which include malnutrition, hormonal imbalances, and irregular heartbeat. The common abuse of laxatives to lose weight can also cause serious damage to body chemistry. Hospitalization is usually required for those who have lost over one-quarter of their normal body weight.

Anorexic teens are often forced into treatment because of the medical problems that stem from starvation. Treatment combines medical monitoring with therapy. Because the anorexic's problems are usually tied in with the family, family counseling is often advised. Nutritional supplements may be prescribed to correct imbalances, and some doctors recommend antidepressants or drugs to control anxiety.

Bulimia

Many teens also suffer from a related eating disorder called bulimia, although it is more common among women in their twenties. It is believed that about one-half of anorexics become bulimic at some point. Bulimia also involves an obsession with food and thinness, but bulimics will overeat and then force themselves to vomit rather than starve themselves. Some young women go back and forth between the two disorders for years.

In a recent study of female high school students, 20 percent reported binge eating (compulsively eating abnormal

amounts of food at one time), and 27 percent described their eating as "out of control." One woman who suffered from bulimia in high school recalls the development of her illness:

> The more I did it, the easier it became. It felt liberating to be able to eat as much as I wanted without worrying about gaining weight. I had no idea I'd slipped onto the path of a disease that would end up dominating my life for the next six years.[20]

Two high school students discuss their studies over lunch. While most teens have healthy attitudes toward eating, for others dieting becomes an obsession and the focus of a serious disease.

Like anorexia, bulimia is strongly associated with depression: 80 percent of those with the eating disorder are estimated to suffer from depression as well. About 20 percent of bulimics attempt suicide, and many become involved with alcohol and drugs. While bulimics are less likely than anorexics to die from their illness, they can develop serious medical problems, including loss of tooth enamel, chemical imbalances, and, in extreme cases, rupture of the esophagus.

Recent studies show bulimics to have low levels of the chemical serotonin in their brains, which is also seen in depression. Because of this, many doctors are now treating the disorder with antidepressants in addition to therapy.

Self-mutilation

A disorder once considered very rare is showing up in increasing numbers of adolescents: self-mutilation, also known as "cutting." People with this disorder cause themselves physical harm by cutting or burning their skin, usually on the forearms between the elbow and wrist.

Self-mutilation typically begins between the ages of eleven and thirteen, and it is three times more common in girls than in boys. Many girls who purposely injure themselves have symptoms of anorexia or drug or alcohol abuse as well, illnesses that also damage the body. They often have a history of physical or sexual abuse.

Teens who self-mutilate describe themselves as feeling "numb," or unable to feel emotion, a common symptom of major depression. Their cutting or burning may be an attempt to feel something, even if that sensation is pain. In the words of one psychiatrist who has studied the disorder, "Someone who feels they are losing touch with reality may grab a knife, scissors, a bottle cap, and the combination of the pain and seeing the blood helps them stop 'disintegrating' mentally."[21]

It is estimated that 1 percent of the American population has this disorder and that they are mostly teens. However, because people who intentionally hurt themselves tend to hide their injuries with long sleeves, self-mutilation may be hard to recognize. When confronted about their wounds, many people will blame them on an accident.

Because it was thought to affect few people until recent years, there is only one center that specializes in the treatment of self-mutilation at this time. Treatment includes antidepressant drugs and various forms of therapy.

Running away

Some depressed teens, convinced their parents don't understand them and full of anger, run away from home. According to a Department of Justice study, between 1 million and 1.5 million American adolescents run away from home each year. They may flee to a city far from home, living on the streets and begging for money. Many become prey to older people who lure them into prostitution, cults, or other criminal activity.

Religious cults and other extremist groups are particularly attractive to adolescents because they provide a substitute home. Those whose own homes are splintered by divorce, alcoholism, or domestic violence often crave the structure these groups offer. As one counselor observes, "Plunging oneself into a group like this represents to these people safety from a confusing and unstable world."[22]

Young people are told what to think and do in these groups. They must live by strict rules that they are not allowed to question. For many teens, who are struggling to define their values and establish a sense of self, this is a relief. They no longer have to think for themselves or make difficult decisions. With their rigid structures and devotion

Depressed teens who feel a lack of understanding from their parents may run away from home out of frustration or anger.

to a single cause, cults may provide distraction from depressed thoughts. However, teens who join them remain stuck in immature ways of thinking. They still feel hopeless underneath and don't develop a sense of self-esteem.

Members of cults and other extremist groups, such as paramilitary organizations and racist "skinhead" gangs, are usually depressed and unable to think for themselves. They shut down their minds and let the group take over. In extreme cases, they may be convinced by cult leaders to commit suicide.

Many other runaways fall into drugs and prostitution. They are offered drugs by people who take advantage of their desperate situation; then, once they are hooked, they need increasing amounts of money to support their habits. Without education or job experience, selling their bodies or stealing may be their only options.

Services for runaway teens

Runaway teens whose situations become desperate may want to come home but fear their parents' reactions to what they have done. Many agencies and organizations were established to help these teens. They often have twenty-four-hour hot lines staffed by trained volunteers, who can refer runaways to social service agencies across the country. There are about five hundred runaway and youth crisis centers in the United States, often providing food, shelter, counseling, and legal help.

Once they have returned to their families, both teens and their parents usually benefit from therapy. It is sometimes necessary to place teens outside the home until problems of physical or sexual abuse are resolved.

Teens who fail to get help for their depression face many dangers. The most serious risk is suicide.

Teen suicide

In a middle-class suburb of Detroit, a high school student, depressed about his failure to graduate with his class, put a gun to his head and ended his life. No one—not even his own family—suspected the depth of the boy's depression. Even more shocking is the fact that he was the third student in his school to commit suicide in four months. Nor would he be the last: Shortly after his death, a fourth student hanged himself.

School counselors reacted quickly to the tragedy, visiting classes to help students share their feelings and express their grief. They sent letters to parents to alert them to warning signs of depression, such as changes in mood, appetite, and sleeping habits or a drop in grades, in their own children. One of the students who received counseling made the observation, "They are saying they did it for attention. I don't think people kill themselves to get attention. I think they do it 'cause they don't think they're worth anything. . . . There's no way out."[23]

Teen suicide is often described as an "epidemic." While this is an exaggeration, the statistics are cause for concern. The rate of suicide for people ages ten to twenty-four has increased by more than 200 percent over the last decade, and suicide is the third leading cause of death for those under twenty-five. Nearly one-third of adolescent deaths are self-inflicted, and teens attempt—and complete—suicide at a much higher rate than do adults.

Detecting suicidal signs is critical. Once a teen has taken an overdose of pills or pulled the trigger, there is seldom a second chance for getting help. Fortunately, most suicidal people do at least hint at their intention, and as many as 90 percent of those who follow through have told someone of their desire to die a week or two before killing themselves.

Another warning sign can be sudden calmness in someone who was very nervous and upset. This sometimes indicates that the person has made the decision to die and feels a sense of peace that the debate is over.

Teens at high risk

Teens at a high risk of suicide often fit a certain profile. They tend to lack strong family ties and frequently have divorced parents. Alcohol and drugs play a major role, and deep depression is almost always part of the picture. According to the Youth Suicide National Center, "the most

---

Common Warning Signs of Suicide

A suicidal person may:

▶ talk about committing suicide

▶ have trouble eating or sleeping

▶ experience drastic changes in behavior

▶ give away prized possessions

▶ have attempted suicide before

▶ take unnecessary risks

▶ have had a recent severe loss

▶ be preoccupied with death and dying

▶ lose interest in personal appearance

▶ increase use of alcohol or drugs

▶ lose interest in hobbies, work, school, etc.

▶ withdraw from friends and/or social activities

▶ prepare for death by making out a will and final arrangements

Source: American Association of Suicidology.

---

common factor is a serious depression, which increasingly is present at younger ages."[24] Suicidal teens are often very intelligent and tend to be high achievers with a strong spirit of competition. Those who experience a break with reality, such as teens with bipolar disorder who have hallucinations, are at particular risk.

Many experts believe environment plays the most important role in the development of suicidal urges. Distrust between parents and children and a lack of family unity make teens more likely to feel lonely and desperate. Parents and teachers often have unrealistic expectations of teens, mistaking physical maturity for emotional maturity.

Some experts observe that many adolescents have not yet developed a realistic view of life, and suicide does not seem real or final to them. The author of a book about a girl who ended her life at age thirteen wrote: "Sometimes, 13-year-olds think that if they kill themselves, everything will be OK; that they'll come back somehow."[25] And a woman who survived to write about her teenage suicide attempt provides this recollection:

Actually, it was only part of myself I wanted to kill: the part that wanted to kill herself, that dragged me into the suicide debate and made every window, kitchen implement, and subway station a rehearsal for tragedy. I didn't figure this out, though, until after I'd swallowed the fifty aspirin.[26]

The events that push a teen over the edge may seem relatively minor. Common triggers are the anticipation of being punished for antisocial behavior or a fight with a parent or a peer of the same sex. Boys, in particular, often have skipped school, committed petty crimes, run away from home, or gotten into fights. There is often a strong feeling of guilt involved.

Teens who have survived a suicide attempt need to be given special attention. Unless their problems are addressed, they are likely to try to end their lives again.

Recognizing teen depression

All experts seem to agree that communication is the key to spotting teen depression. Since many teenagers are reluctant to ask for help, the American Medical Association (AMA) recommends that health professionals question them annually about any behaviors or feelings that hint at the disease. AMA guidelines advise screening teens who show a drop in school grades, problems within the family, homosexual orientation, physical or sexual abuse, alcohol or drug use, or a previous suicide attempt. Teens whose problems relate to their families will be reluctant to approach a parent for help, so talking to a doctor, teacher, school counselor, or coach is often a better option. In order to share difficult emotions, teens must find an adult they feel they can trust.

4

Treating Depression

DEPRESSION IS CONSIDERED one of the most treatable diseases of the mind. There are a wide variety of treatments available today, including several forms of talk and behavior therapy and a rapidly growing number of drugs. The standard forms of treatment are often used in combination, and it sometimes takes experimenting to find the best treatment for an individual.

Psychoanalysis

Modern methods of treating depression began in the late nineteenth century with Sigmund Freud, a Viennese physician. When many people think of psychiatrists, they see the popular image of Freud: a stern, elderly bearded man with a thick German accent, smoking a pipe in a corner of his office while his patient lies on a couch. Few psychiatrists today continue to use the form of treatment developed by Freud. However, his ideas have had a lasting impact on the field of psychiatry.

Freud was the founder of psychoanalysis, a method of treating mental illness by helping patients discover and face the causes of their disease. (The word comes from the Greek *psyche,* meaning "the mind," and *analysis,* "a separation of the whole into parts.") The psychiatrist, or analyst, believes that these causes are buried deep in the patient's unconscious and can be brought out by "free associating"— saying whatever comes to mind during the session. The treatment typically takes many years, with the patient having several one-hour sessions a week with the analyst.

The theories of Freud

Freud's theory was that all humans have unconscious thoughts that strongly affect their behavior. When there is a conflict among these thoughts, or when they go against conscious ideas of right and wrong, they cause emotional problems. Freud believed that people's early childhood experiences have the most important influence in shaping their personalities, thoughts, feelings, and behavior. He also believed that the thoughts buried in the subconscious usually involve sex or violence and are therefore forbidden. The job of the analyst was to help patients feel safe to uncover these hidden memories.

In Freud's system, the mind is broken down into three areas: the id, the ego, and the superego. The id is the part that holds primitive thoughts and urges—the ones that would not be acceptable to express in society. The superego is the conscience, the part of the mind that keeps people from expressing these thoughts and feelings (or makes them feel guilt if they do). The ego's role is to mediate between the id and the superego, to help people reach a healthy balance between acting out their impulses and shutting down their feelings.

In classical psychoanalysis, the analyst was a distant figure who basically sat back and listened while the patient on the couch said whatever came to mind. The idea was to interrupt only when the patient seemed ready to recognize important thoughts rising from the unconscious. Over time, the patient would come to act toward the analyst as if he or she were a parent, transferring childhood feelings to this substitute father or mother.

The psychoanalytic view of depression

Psychoanalysts see depression as a problem in coming to terms with loss. All people experience a period of mourning after a loss, but most learn to work through it and accept the loss. Depressed people, however, are preoccupied with loss. Their feelings of sadness and grief take over their lives, preventing them from responding to positive

Psychoanalysis has largely been replaced by group therapy and other forms of counseling in the treatment of depression.

events. In adolescence, loss can be the loss of childhood and everything being a child permits. Teens must give up their protected roles as children and take on the responsibility of becoming an adult.

Traditional psychoanalysts believe that boys, fearing their father's rivalry, are forced to give up their desire for their mother's total attention and love. They feel guilt about their anger toward their father. The inner struggle over their changing feelings toward their parents changes their personalities and leads them to develop a conscience (the superego). As they mature, boys grow to identify with the father.

In girls, the process is a little different. They are dependent on the mother but also have a growing need for the father's approval and love. They find themselves becoming the mother's rival for the father's attention. Eventually they come to identify with the mother.

Adolescence is seen as a time when boys and girls are trying to separate from their parents to establish their own identities in the outside world. If the process is too sudden or if children reject their parents' values too quickly, they may experience feelings of guilt, a loss of self-esteem, and depression.

Changing views toward psychoanalysis

Psychoanalysis was extremely popular in the United States during the 1940s and 1950s. It was widely considered the most effective treatment for all disorders of the mind. It first came under attack in the 1960s, when feminists criticized the male-dominated field and questioned many of its concepts (one of which was that girls had a secret envy of boys). In the 1970s, the development of new drugs to treat mood disorders, which worked much more quickly and inexpensively, struck a second blow to psychoanalysis. And in the 1980s, insurance companies began refusing to pay for the expensive long-term treatment, forcing many patients to seek alternatives.

Today, psychoanalysis continues on a much smaller scale and with modified techniques. Most analysts who still accept Freud's principles practice variations of the technique, in which patients have fewer sessions, sit in chairs, and receive more direction and feedback from the analyst. Also, most analysts now agree that psychoanalysis is not the best treatment for many mood disorders. It does not seem to work well for people with bipolar disorder, eating disorders, or alcohol or drug abuse problems. People with severe depression do better with therapies that offer more interaction with the therapist.

Newer forms of psychotherapy

Psychotherapy is a general term for a variety of treatments that have the relationship between patient and therapist at their center. While many psychotherapists still follow the basic teachings of Freud, they may use very different techniques to help people resolve their emotional problems.

Most forms of psychotherapy today have both an immediate and a long-term goal. The immediate goal is to relieve the discomfort and stress that prevent the patient from functioning effectively. The long-term goal is to change the person's self-defeating patterns of thinking, feeling, and acting.

Modern therapies for depression usually start with a supportive approach. They aim to help people deal with immediate problems that interfere with their day-to-day lives. Once the patient is functioning better, they go on to

People afflicted with depression often find psychotherapy to be a crucial part of their treatment.

explore the issues that cause the negative patterns of be-havior. This is often called a psychodynamic approach.

Psychodynamic therapy

The two main forms of psychodynamic therapy are brief dynamic therapy and interpersonal therapy. Brief dynamic therapy is more similar to traditional psychoanalysis, though the therapist takes a more active role. It is also much briefer than psychoanalysis, usually lasting fewer than thirty sessions. Interpersonal therapy focuses on im-proving the patient's close relationships, using the relation-ship with the therapist as a model. It was developed specifically to treat depression and is considered very ef-fective.

Psychotherapists usually meet with their patients twice a week early in treatment, then weekly once the patient's symptoms are under control. A good therapist is always available to patients in crisis or has a partner covering when he or she cannot be reached.

Other forms of therapy focus less on the causes of de-pression and more on changing the thoughts and actions that keep people from enjoying life. The main types are cognitive and behavioral therapies.

Cognitive and behavioral therapies

Cognitive and behavioral therapies take a very different approach to treating illness of the mind than does psy-chotherapy. Their focus is on the present rather than the past, and their goal is to change negative behavior rather than understand how it developed over the years.

Behavioral therapy began with experiments on animals proving that they learn how to act based on rewards and punishments. When a certain type of behavior was re-warded, the animals repeated it; when another behavior was punished, they avoided it. Later studies on humans showed similar results. The main idea behind behavioral therapy is that people who are rewarded for the wrong things and punished for positive acts end up behaving in ways that don't serve them well. A behavioral therapist analyzes a person's behavior and determines what is causing it to continue, then works with the person to change it.

Cognitive therapy is a more recent technique that is often used with behavioral therapy. Cognitive therapists believe that the types of thoughts a person typically has determine how that person feels and acts. They study and explain people's negative thinking patterns and how these patterns lead to symptoms of illness. The main goal is the reduction of symptoms.

A practical approach

Both behavioral and cognitive therapies take a direct, practical approach to treatment. They teach patients better habits to relieve depression and other illnesses within a short period of time. Treatment may involve only ten or twelve sessions and seldom lasts more than six months.

The main premise of both these therapies is that whatever has been learned can be unlearned. At the beginning of treatment, the therapist and patient usually draw up a list of the behaviors the patient wants to change. Patients agree to keep logs of their behavior, thoughts, and attempts to change them. This trains them to monitor the ways they think and act. As one doctor describes it, "Ultimately, the goal of behavior therapy is that the patient should become her own therapist, able to use all of the techniques learned on her own to quickly reverse impending relapse."[27]

To test how well treatment is working, cognitive and behavioral therapists often use rating scales. They grade the severity of each of the patient's symptoms at the beginning of treatment and then again during treatment to compare scores. Unlike psychoanalysts, they look for reportable, objective signs of improvement.

Psychoanalysts view this kind of treatment as superficial, since it focuses on symptoms rather than causes. In their view, the symptoms will recur if the underlying cause of the illness has not been treated. However, behavioral and cognitive therapists would say that there is no way of proving the causes of a mood disorder, and they give the patient tools to deal with symptoms if they come back.

Disorders that respond well

Cognitive and behavioral therapies tend to be very effective in treating mild depression, drug and alcohol abuse, and bulimia. They are usually incorporated in substance abuse programs, particularly twelve-step programs such as Alcoholics Anonymous and Narcotics Anonymous. The techniques are less helpful in treating major depression and bipolar disorder, which both respond better to drug therapy.

Many teens do well with these forms of therapy. Since they tend to be reluctant to discuss—or even admit—their problems, a treatment in which therapist and patient both play active roles is usually easier for them than traditional psychoanalysis. Also, a goal of getting results quickly is more likely to appeal to teens, who are often short on patience.

Many depressed teens—especially those with substance abuse problems—also find group therapy useful. Therapy groups usually focus on particular problems shared by their members.

Group therapy

Group therapy has been used for many years to treat addictions. One of the most successful programs is Alcoholics Anonymous, which has helped millions of people addicted to alcohol stop drinking. A similar program to fight drug addiction, Narcotics Anonymous, uses the same approach. Both organizations run some meetings exclusively for teens.

In these groups, people with the same disorder meet regularly to share their experiences and offer one another support. They all have the same goal: staying away from the addictive substance. Such groups are known as being "task-oriented," since they have very specific guidelines and goals.

The success of these programs has encouraged people with other depression-related disorders, such as compulsive eating, to form similar groups. Here, the task is a little more complicated, since people can't avoid eating, as they can alcohol or drugs. However, group programs like Overeaters Anonymous have shown success in helping people control their eating disorders.

Advantages and drawbacks

Other types of therapy groups deal with illnesses that have a wider range of symptoms, such as major depression. These are usually run by a therapist who specializes in treating the disorder. For people with depression, who often experience social withdrawal, a therapy group may provide a sense of community and support. Many people feel alone in their illness, and just knowing they are not the only one struggling with certain feelings and symptoms is often helpful.

One of the advantages of group therapy is its cost. The twelve-step programs for addictions are free, and therapist-run groups are usually much less expensive than individual therapy. Another advantage is having a network of people

Group therapy is especially successful in treating depression-related problems such as drug addiction and eating disorders.

with similar problems who can offer advice and support. A possible disadvantage is that people may become dependent on groups and use them as a substitute for interacting with the outside world. Also, those who need additional treatment, such as antidepressants or individual therapy, may believe that the group can take its place.

The most successful groups seem to be those whose members share the same clear, specific goals, such as staying away from an addictive substance or breaking a self-defeating habit. Groups that combine people with a variety of problems may help their members interact better, but they won't provide much treatment for their individual illnesses.

Group therapy can be very effective in helping teens, especially those struggling with drug or alcohol problems. Some of these groups are designed specifically for teens, since they are likely to feel most comfortable among their peers. This setting encourages them to share feelings and concerns that they find hard to discuss with adults. A woman whose bipolar disorder began in her teens describes her experience with group therapy:

> I found out about what is now the National Depressive and Manic-Depressive Association (DMDA), at the time just a local support group, and two days after I got out of the hospital I went to a meeting. Each sentence I started, someone in the group could finish. It felt wonderful to be among people who understood what I'd been through.[28]

All types of therapy can be used along with antidepressant drugs. Doctors who once seldom prescribed them for teens now see their benefits for depressed patients of all ages.

Antidepressants

Drugs for treating mood disorders have been around for more than thirty years, but it is only recently that researchers have come to understand how they work. This knowledge has led to the development of many effective new psychiatric drugs, particularly for depression.

Before 1970, few doctors believed that drugs could fight depression effectively. Psychotherapy was still the standard form of treatment for the disease. However, the high cost of psychoanalysis was beyond the reach of most Americans, so more and more doctors began prescribing antidepressants. By the 1970s these drugs were being widely used, and doctors were accepting the fact that depression is at least partly a biological disease.

Today, all but the most traditional psychoanalysts consider antidepressants to be effective in treating many depressed patients. Unlike other forms of therapy, the success of drugs in treating mood disorders is scientifically proven. Before a new antidepressant is approved for use in the United States, the Food and Drug Administration requires substantial proof that it works. Scientists must do extensive studies in which half the participants are given the drug and the other half a placebo, a sugar pill that looks exactly like the drug being tested. The studies are "double-blind," meaning that neither the doctor nor the test participants know who is taking the placebo.

Learning how these drugs work is helping researchers develop safer and more effective antidepressants. Recent advances in the study of brain chemistry are increasing the treatment options for depression.

How they work

Though there is still a lot to discover, scientists have made great strides in the last few years toward understanding how the brain controls mood. The brain is made up of millions of cells called neurons, which send messages to each other through connectors called axons. Information passes between the neurons much like electrical current. For this information to reach across the spaces between the neurons, known as synapses, the neurons must manufacture chemicals called neurotransmitters.

Most psychiatric drugs, including antidepressants, influence the way neurotransmitters work. Different neurons use different neurotransmitters to send messages. When a neurotransmitter binds to a receptor on the next neuron, it causes a chemical reaction in the new cell, allowing the signal to be sent to another neuron. This process allows the different parts of the brain to communicate with each other.

Any disturbance in this complex process can lead to a disturbance in mood. Scientists have identified certain neurotransmitters that appear to play important roles in depression. The two that seem most important are norepinephrine and serotonin. The new antidepressants work on one or both of these chemicals, helping them bind effectively with their receptors.

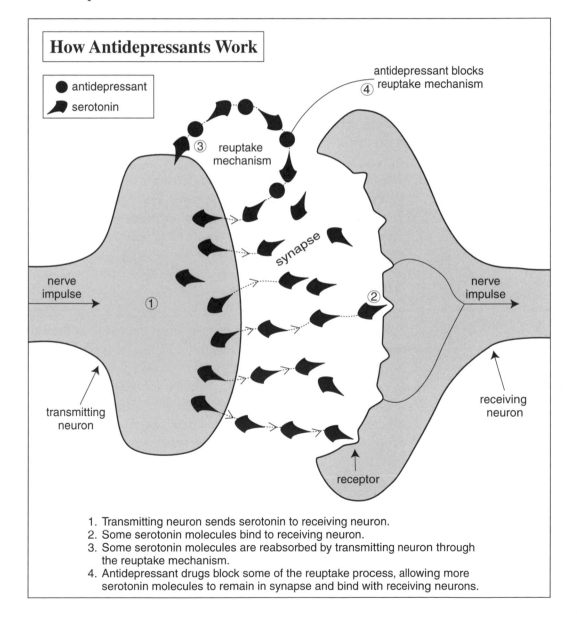

How Antidepressants Work

● antidepressant
serotonin

antidepressant blocks reuptake mechanism
④

③ reuptake mechanism

synapse

nerve impulse

①

②

nerve impulse

transmitting neuron

receiving neuron

receptor

1. Transmitting neuron sends serotonin to receiving neuron.
2. Some serotonin molecules bind to receiving neuron.
3. Some serotonin molecules are reabsorbed by transmitting neuron through the reuptake mechanism.
4. Antidepressant drugs block some of the reuptake process, allowing more serotonin molecules to remain in synapse and bind with receiving neurons.

Many experts believe that serotonin has the greatest impact on depression. Lack of this chemical appears to increase irritability, aggression, impulsive behavior, the rate of violent suicide, alcohol and drug use, compulsive eating, and insomnia. Serotonin actually seems to have a cooling effect on the brain, and some doctors believe that what is commonly referred to as "stress" is an increase in body temperature.

Types of antidepressants

Several antidepressants work directly on serotonin. These are called selective serotonin reuptake inhibitors, or SSRIs. This group of drugs includes Prozac, Zoloft, and Paxil. All three are similar, but some people respond to one better than the others.

The two other major groups of antidepressants are tricyclics and monoamine oxidase inhibitors, or MAOIs. Tricyclics focus on two neurotransmitters, serotonin and norepinephrine. They elevate mood by keeping these chemicals active longer. However, they also tend to affect neurotransmitters that they are not targeting. This often causes unpleasant side effects, including drowsiness, dry mouth and eyes, sensitivity to light, blurred vision, constipation, and weight gain.

MAOIs block the enzyme monoamine oxidase, making more brain chemicals available. They are seldom recommended for teens. In addition to causing side effects, MAOIs have dangerous interactions with certain foods, including cheese and beans, and so require following a special diet. Eating these foods while taking the drug can cause steep increases in blood pressure. Many teens have a hard time tolerating the side effects or watching what they eat, and they stop taking these drugs. The drugs generally are prescribed for teens only when SSRIs fail to work.

Some studies have shown that adolescents don't respond as well as adults to antidepressants. Research suggests that their neurotransmitters may not be fully developed. However, a recent study of one of the most popular SSRIs, Prozac, shows that it is as effective for treating depression

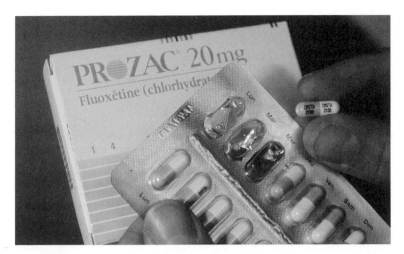

The antidepressant Prozac has been shown to be an effective treatment for depression in adolescents.

in children and teens as in adults. Among young people who took the drug for two months, 56 percent were rated "much improved" or "very much improved" and 74 percent showed some improvement in symptoms. There was no difference in response between boys and girls.

The SSRIs usually take four to six weeks to work completely. Unfortunately, most side effects show up before the positive effects of the drug are felt. Many teens become impatient about feeling worse before they start to feel better and stop taking the drug. Since most side effects tend to go away over time, patience is rewarded.

Fears about antidepressants

Many people fear that antidepressants will change their personalities and that they will no longer be "themselves." However, in the words of one doctor who spent years studying the new drugs, "what emerges is the patient's true personality, which the illness had previously smothered."[29] In most cases, the change people experience is not dramatic and is noticed only over time.

A woman who was helped by antidepressants notes,

> I felt for the first time in my life, my "real" personality had emerged. Going on the medication did so much more than I expected. The only thing that marred this rebirth was the thought that I had wasted so many years living in the fog of depression.[30]

Another woman taking antidepressants observes: "My progress, as with any chronic condition, has been neither smooth nor rapid, but it has been steadily uphill."[31]

Another common fear is of side effects. All antidepressants can cause unpleasant side effects, although these often go away once the body adjusts to its new chemistry. For most people, the SSRIs have fewer side effects than the other groups of drugs. However, Prozac can cause such symptoms as nausea, headaches, sleeplessness, loss of appetite, and nervousness, which is why some newer SSRIs are recommended for many people. When side effects occur, doctors often try reducing the dosage.

Many people fear that antidepressants will have the same addictive qualities as most recreational drugs. However, they are very different in nature. People don't get "high" on antidepressants; they simply don't experience the same lows as when they are depressed. Antidepressants are not addictive either. People who stop taking them don't crave them. They may have some withdrawal symptoms if they stop too suddenly, but these can be controlled by tapering off under a doctor's supervision.

The fear that taking drugs to control a mood disorder is a sign of weakness is losing ground. As more and more people recognize that depression has biological causes, they are becoming less resistant to making chemical cor-

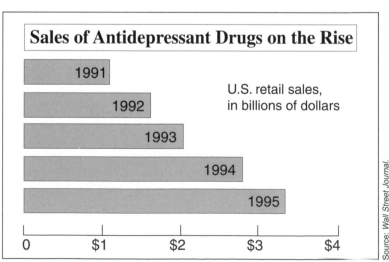

Sales of Antidepressant Drugs on the Rise

U.S. retail sales, in billions of dollars

1991
1992
1993
1994
1995

0    $1 $2 $3 $4

Source: Wall Street Journal.

rections to the way the brain works. Treating depression is becoming more like treating an infection or injury.

Who should take antidepressants?

Antidepressants are the preferred form of treatment for conditions that require immediate relief. Any situation that puts a person in danger calls for a fast response. This includes suicidal thinking, hallucinations, inability to eat or sleep, and violent behavior. People who are in danger of harming themselves or others cannot wait for a treatment that takes months or years to work.

For most other forms of depression, people have a choice. Mild depression can be treated with drugs, psychoanalysis, cognitive or behavioral therapy, or any combination. If antidepressants are used to treat alcohol or drug addiction, an additional form of therapy is almost always required.

A recent study of adolescents shows that antidepressants work best for those with a family history of major depression. Teens whose parents don't show signs of the disease had much poorer results, and the researchers concluded that they would respond better to cognitive, behavioral, or group therapy.

More and more doctors are prescribing antidepressants, often without combining them with other forms of treatment. Studies show that antidepressants work best when the patient is also receiving some other type of therapy. It is also important for doctors to monitor people taking antidepressants for side effects and the need to adjust dosage. Many people are prescribed amounts that are too small to make a difference in the way they feel.

While therapy and antidepressants can help most depressed people, some are paralyzed by such extreme depression that they need a faster solution. For such people, the quickest and most effective treatment may be electroconvulsive therapy.

Electroconvulsive therapy

Because of the bad image it has developed through the media, electroconvulsive therapy, or ECT, is no longer a common treatment for depression. Better known as "shock treatment," ECT applies an electric shock of about eighty volts through electrodes to the head. The patient is given anesthesia, so the shock is not felt. The treatment is usually given three times a week for two weeks and seldom goes beyond ten sessions.

ECT was frequently misused in its early years. Doctors often used it for disorders it wasn't designed to treat. It was also used in mental hospitals as a threat to control difficult patients, and many people received too many treatments.

Although people tend to think of ECT as a dangerous form of treatment, it is actually quite safe. It is also one of the most effective ways of treating depression, with a success rate between 80 and 90 percent for patients with major depression or bipolar disorder. Despite dramatic movie scenes showing patients given shock treatment against their will, it is now used only with a patient's consent. However, because it generally requires hospitalization and remains a controversial method, ECT is usually reserved for people with severe or suicidal depression who fail to respond to other treatment.

No one is certain how ECT works. However, its effectiveness encouraged researchers to seek biological causes for depression in the brain, leading to the development of many antidepressant drugs.

Hospitalization

Some mental disorders, including severe depression, may at times require hospitalization. Years ago, people with serious psychiatric problems were often hospitalized against their will. Today, however, very few hospitalizations for mental illness are involuntary.

People with severe mood disorders can still be admitted to hospitals without giving their consent only if they appear to be in serious danger of harming themselves or others. This would include those who are suicidal or violent. Most people must be brought to an emergency room before being admitted, and a doctor must determine that they are in real danger. This type of hospital admission usually involves the police or an ambulance.

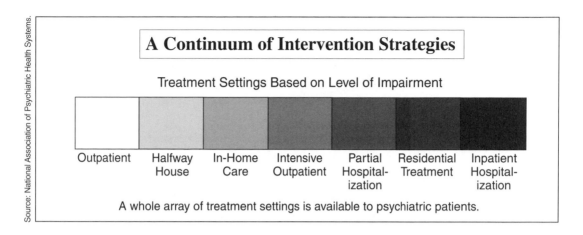

A Continuum of Intervention Strategies

Treatment Settings Based on Level of Impairment

| Outpatient | Halfway House | In-Home Care | Intensive Outpatient | Partial Hospital-ization | Residential Treatment | Inpatient Hospital-ization |

A whole array of treatment settings is available to psychiatric patients.

Many hospitalizations for mood disorders are voluntary. In these cases, the patient, doctor, and patient's family all agree that there is no other place where the patient can get the treatment he or she needs in order to recover. Voluntary admissions are often for drug or alcohol addictions, anorexia nervosa, or bipolar disorder, conditions that may require supervised medical treatment.

Hospitalization can take someone out of a stressful environment and give that person time to break a cycle of negative behavior. When this involves painful withdrawal from drugs or alcohol, hospitals offer medical support and supervision that makes the process easier and safer. For an anorexic near starvation, hospital care can restore nutrients and reverse dangerous weight loss.

For people hospitalized for diseases of the mind, the hospital stay is usually only the first step on the road to recovery. Follow-up therapy is needed to keep the addiction or other disorder from coming back. Many hospitals provide outpatient programs, where former patients can be monitored and continue to receive treatment.

The therapeutic relationship

A recent study compared several types of therapy for depression—psychoanalysis, cognitive and behavior therapies, and treatment with antidepressant drugs—to see whether the form of treatment or the relationship between the patient and therapist was more important. All forms of therapy showed similar results. With each type of treatment, the patients who showed the greatest improvement were those who had a good relationship with their therapist. The study concluded that the quality of the patient-therapist relationship, not the form of treatment, played the most important role in the therapy's success.

The patient-therapist relationship is especially important in the treatment of depressed teens. Most teens are more reluctant to discuss their problems than are adults and more resistant to people who try to help. While adults usually choose their own therapists, teens' doctors are generally chosen by their parents. Teens may resent their parents' interference in their lives and transfer these feelings to the therapist.

Because depressed teens may be reluctant to discuss their problems with adults, finding a therapist they trust is often a critical part of recovery.

Finding a therapist a teenager can trust and feel comfortable with may be the most important step in treating teen depression. Teens must feel that they have a safe place where they can talk freely and that whatever they say will be held in confidence. They need a therapist who can be supportive while offering a new perspective on the teen's thoughts, feelings, and actions.

Finding a therapist

There are several ways to locate a good therapist. Family doctors often make referrals, particularly in the case of teens. Knowing a teen's family is an advantage in choosing a therapist who can help with his or her particular problems.

Professional organizations are also good sources of information. The American Psychiatric Association, the American Psychological Association, and the National Association of Social Workers can recommend psychiatrists, psychologists, and social workers certified to practice in each state. Unfortunately, practically anyone can practice psychotherapy. There is no professional license required, although many people who practice are licensed in their own field, such as psychiatry or psychology. For this reason, it is usually best to choose a therapist who belongs to one of these professional groups.

Choosing a therapist

Teens who are not comfortable with a therapist should express this to their parents. There are many therapists with many different approaches, and it may be necessary to consult with several before making a choice.

A therapist's personality and values are important factors in the relationship with the patient. Some people are more comfortable opening up to a therapist who is talkative and asks a lot of questions; others prefer a quiet listener. Some want a more formal relationship than others. Many teens feel it is important for the therapist to accept them as they are, but some prefer to be challenged.

The therapist's sex is sometimes an issue, as many teens feel more comfortable talking to someone of the same sex.

Members of minority groups often feel that a therapist of their own race or nationality will understand them better. People who are gay or lesbian may prcfer a therapist of their sexual orientation, or at least one with experience working with homosexual patients. Feeling that a therapist is not prejudiced is very important, especially for teens who are in the process of establishing their identities.

Finding the best treatment—or combination of treatments—for a particular teen's depression often takes some time and effort. Teens need to give their therapy or medication a chance to work. They must also be willing to change treatments if a particular form isn't relieving their symptoms over a reasonable amount of time. The right therapist or antidepressant can have a major impact on a young person's life.

5

Alternative Treatments

MANY PEOPLE WHO are uncomfortable with drugs or traditional forms of therapy try alternative treatments. These include any substance or procedure that is out of the medical mainstream.

Alternative treatments have been used for mood disorders for years. Some, in fact, go back to ancient times. They cover a wide range, from inhaling natural oils to taking mixtures of herbs to meditating. Though few scientific studies have been done to prove how well they work, many people have found them helpful for mild depression. They can be used alongside more traditional forms of treatment to increase their effectiveness.

Treatments that can be traced back for centuries include acupuncture, massage therapy, reflexology, herbal therapies, and homeopathic medicine. The first four were developed in ancient times; homeopathy was introduced in the medieval era. All have been experiencing renewed interest in recent years, especially among the young.

Acupuncture

Acupuncture has been used for thousands of years in China to treat hundreds of diseases, and it has recently become popular in the West. It uses an ancient Chinese map of the body in which there are fourteen meridians, or energy channels. When these channels become blocked, acupuncturists believe, symptoms of disease develop. To

stimulate the blocked energy channels, acupuncturists use
very thin needles at any of 365 points on the body. Some
also use "pulling cups," glass suction cups that pull up the
skin on points on the lower back that correspond to the
blocked organ.

Though Western doctors doubted its effectiveness for
years, acupuncture is now becoming widely accepted in
the United States. A panel of scientists at the National In-
stitutes of Health recently agreed that it works for a number of conditions. The doctor who chaired the panel
observed: "Acupuncture has fewer side effects and is less
invasive than many of the other things we do in conventional Western medicine. It's time to take it seriously."[32]
The panel recommended that medical insurance start covering the procedure for certain illnesses. The World Health
Organization has endorsed the use of acupuncture to treat
about forty ailments.

The Food and Drug Administration estimates that as
many as 12 million Americans have received acupuncture
treatment from about ten thousand doctors or licensed acu-

puncture practitioners. Most of them tried it when other forms of treatment failed to relieve their symptoms.

Recent studies show that acupuncture taps into the body's natural protective and pain-fighting system. It increases brain activity, boosts the immune system, and releases pain-fighting chemicals. Its effectiveness in treating depression is less certain, though many people say it has helped relieve symptoms of the disease, including sleep disorders.

Massage therapy

Most people in the West think of massage as something that simply relaxes tense muscles. In traditional Chinese medicine, however, it is used much like acupuncture. Doctors in China use massage to treat all types of imbalances in the body, including those thought to cause depression. They locate pressure points that relate to the systems under stress. As one massage doctor describes it, "Through

While no studies have yet proven medical massage to be an effective treatment for depression, American doctors are beginning to explore its usefulness when combined with traditional treatments.

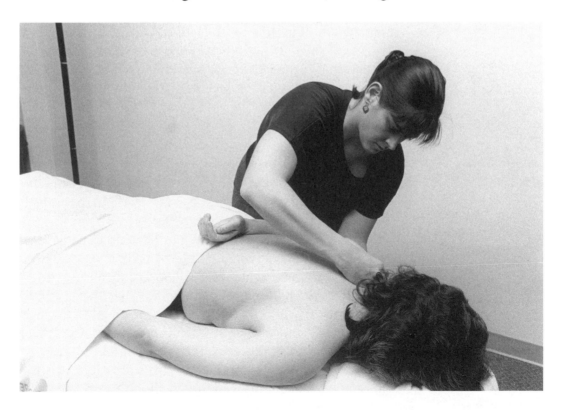

proper reconditioning of one's meridians, both internal and external diseases can be cured."[33]

Medical massage is becoming popular in the United States as well, although its effectiveness for disorders like depression is just beginning to be studied.

Reflexology

First used thousands of years ago, reflexology is a technique that has been recently revived. It is a form of deep massage, usually of pressure points on the hands or feet.

As with acupuncture, people who practice reflexology believe that different points on the body correspond to various body systems. Reflexology divides the body into ten zones that relate to the ten fingers or toes. Practitioners locate the spot on the hand or foot that is connected to pain or disturbance in another part of the body.

Reflexologists view depression as a disorder that compresses the body's energy field. To treat it, they often do a general massage of the foot that is supposed to balance the immune and hormone systems and relax the spine. They try to stimulate circulation and release blocked energy.

There is little evidence to prove that reflexology works, but some people claim it has helped them with symptoms of depression.

Herbal therapies

Herbs have been used for thousands of years to treat a wide variety of illnesses, both of the body and of the mind. Some of the more popular herbal therapies are St. John's wort and combinations of Chinese herbs.

St. John's wort is an herb that has been used as far back as ancient Greece to treat a number of ailments, including depression. Its Greek name, *hypericum,* means "over an apparition"—a reference to the belief that it scared evil spirits away.

While St. John's wort has been used in the past to heal wounds, as well as illnesses of the kidneys and lungs, its main use today is in the treatment of depression. It is the most thoroughly researched and used herb ever to treat a mood disorder. In Germany, where it has been used for this purpose longer than in the United States, more than 20 million people are taking it regularly. More than five thousand people have participated in studies of the herb's effectiveness for depression. The results show that St. John's wort works as well as many prescription antidepressants. Between 50 and 80 percent of people observed showed a significant drop in depressive symptoms.

The usual recommended dosage of St. John's wort is three hundred milligrams taken in capsules three times a day. Though it is also available as a tea, no studies have been done to test its effectiveness in this form. Like prescription antidepressants, it works gradually, so people may not notice much improvement before six weeks.

The advantages of St. John's wort over antidepressant drugs are that no prescription is needed, the cost is lower, and there are few reported side effects. It is available in most health food stores and many drugstores. However, studies on the herb are not as extensive as those on prescription drugs. Also, because it is not tested by the Food and Drug Administration (since it is considered a "dietary supplement" rather than a drug), there is no guarantee that one brand is as effective as another.

Because teens often suffer side effects from antidepressant drugs, St. John's wort may offer a good alternative. However, it is not recommended as a substitute for other treatment for severe depression.

Chinese herbs

Herbal remedies are at the center of ancient Chinese medicine, which is still widely practiced in China today. The Chinese system of herbal treatment, developed twenty-five hundred years ago, is based on the principle of *ch'i*, the body's energy or life force. Though the theory of *ch'i* is unrelated to Western understanding of the body, many American doctors are now studying ancient Chinese treatments.

Traditional Chinese hospitals have large herbal pharmacies that combine various herbs to brew teas for each patient's illness. There are about two thousand different herbs

An herbalist prepares a remedy in a Chinese pharmacy. Some American doctors are now studying these ancient Chinese treatments as alternatives to traditional Western medicine.

that can be used, and a typical preparation contains ten to fifteen herbs that are steeped for about a half hour. Each dose of herbal medicine is freshly prepared for the patient. These herbal mixtures are believed to increase or decrease the amount of *ch'i* that is blocking one of the body's systems and causing disease. Traditional Chinese doctors look for imbalances in the patient's energy channels and find combinations of herbs that restore the normal flow of energy.

Though there are no scientific studies to prove the theory of *ch'i,* ancient Chinese remedies seem to have helped millions of people. Eastern medicine does not make a distinction between diseases of the mind and those of the body, so depression is considered one of the many symptoms of an imbalance in a person's energy fields.

Western herbalists are beginning to practice many Chinese herbal remedies. They may combine Chinese and Western herbs that are believed to help the symptoms of depression, such as lack of sleep or loss of appetite. There are also preparations of Chinese herbs sold at many health food stores. However, no scientific studies have been done to prove their effectiveness.

Homeopathic medicine

Other natural remedies with a long history of use are homeopathic treatments. Homeopathy is a system of medicine that uses highly diluted substances to encourage the body to heal itself. It has been used more widely in Europe than in the United States but has grown more popular here in recent years. Most health food stores now carry a variety of homeopathic remedies.

First used in medieval times, homeopathic medicine was revived about two hundred years ago and now uses a combination of old and modern cures. The substances it uses come from plants, animals, minerals, chemicals, and conventional drugs. Homeopathy seems to work well for some people and not at all for others. It is sometimes effective for symptoms of depression.

Diet and nutrition

While many doctors doubt the effects of most natural treatments on depression, few will argue against the benefits of diet and exercise on mood. Scientific studies are now proving that a balanced diet and active lifestyle help relieve depressive symptoms.

In addition to harming general health, poor nutrition makes the symptoms of depression worse. Dieters suffer from depression more than others, since most diets are lacking in important nutrients. Teens are especially prone to following poor diets, and those with eating disorders such as anorexia may develop serious malnutrition.

Many dieters lack vitamins needed for good brain function. Vitamin C is needed to make serotonin, and B6 helps raise serotonin function. Vitamin E deficiency can interfere with the working of the neuron system in the brain. Several minerals aid the functioning of serotonin, including magnesium, zinc, copper, manganese, and iron.

While most people worry about high cholesterol, which contributes to heart disease, very low cholesterol has been linked to depression. People with extremely low cholesterol levels also have low serotonin levels. Levels below 160 milligrams have been associated with a high risk of suicide.

Despite the nation's focus on dieting and cutting down on fat, Americans are heavier than ever. About one-third are overweight, and many—particularly teenage girls—try to lose the extra weight with unhealthy, unbalanced diets that may be contributing to their depression.

Exercise

Even doctors who doubt the benefits of all other alternative treatments recommend exercise for people with depression. It improves the flow of blood to the brain, raises mood, and helps relieve stress.

Exercise raises the body's level of serotonin, the chemical that seems to have the greatest effect on regulating mood. Studies have shown that a ninety-minute workout on a treadmill can double a person's serotonin level. Thirty minutes of jogging three times a week seems to be as effective as psychotherapy in treating moderate depression.

New research suggests that certain types of exercise—those that involve repetitive movement—increase serotonin levels more than others. In people who exercise regularly over a period of time, high serotonin activity appears to last for weeks after the exercise is stopped. A recent study shows that only 37 percent of high school students are getting even moderate amounts of regular exercise. This lack of activity may be contributing to teen depression.

While scientific evidence of the benefits of exercise is new, people have recognized its positive effects for thousands of years. In China, people have been practicing martial arts for twenty-three hundred years to prevent and treat illness of the body and mind. The aim is to center the body's energy and shift it to wherever it is needed to maintain balance and health. The exercises use pulling and pushing movements to control the body's energy flow. Even many of the elderly practice them every day.

Tai chi chuan is practiced by millions in China and is becoming popular in the West. According to a Chinese doctor, "The true purpose is to seek harmony with the world and with oneself, which is what Chinese medicine is really meant for."[34]

Because stress can trigger depression, doctors recommend regular exercise for managing stress. Aerobic exercise may also have positive effects on mood.

Other natural treatments seek to restore the body's natural rhythms, which have been thrown out of balance by modern life. These include light therapy and melatonin.

Light therapy

Light therapy, also known as phototherapy, has been used successfully to treat seasonal affective disorder, or winter depression. Some studies show that it may be helpful for other types of depression as well.

Since early humans had long exposure to the sunlight, many researchers believe that the brain has trouble adapting to the unnatural darkness of modern life. In the words of one, "We have lost our strongest connection with the daily rhythm of nature."[35]

Early forms of light therapy go back to the ancient Greeks. In the early twentieth century, doctors used light for both medical and psychiatric purposes. Many hospitals had solariums where patients could be exposed to light.

A woman with seasonal affective disorder begins her day by reading in front of a light box. Exposure to light has been shown to increase levels of serotonin, which may elevate mood.

However, the discovery of drugs to treat depression created a loss of interest in light therapy. Then, in the 1980s, studies showed that people have a hormonal response to light, and doctors began to use it to treat winter depression.

Light has been shown to boost serotonin and energy levels. Recent research suggests that the pineal gland in the brains of many people is sensitive to the loss of light, causing depression during the darker months. Many people report relief from using light boxes or lights attached to helmets in winter.

While people can purchase light boxes to use at home, light therapy works best under trained supervision. Too little light has no effect, and too much can cause side effects, including mild symptoms of mania.

Melatonin

Melatonin is a hormone that helps people adapt to basic environmental rhythms, such as sleeping at night and awakening in the morning. Because of this, many people have been taking it to get to sleep. It also appears to fight stress by calming the nervous system.

Since sleeplessness and stress are often symptoms of depression, some people are taking melatonin to fight depressed moods. Low levels of melatonin have been found in people addicted to alcohol, as well as in those with premenstrual syndrome and seasonal affective disorder.

Melatonin supplements are widely available in health food stores and many drugstores. However, because they have not done testing to prove its safety and effectiveness, the Food and Drug Administration has been trying to stop its sale. Since it is not regulated as a drug, the doses and purity of the product may vary widely.

Some researchers are advising against self-medication with the supplements. They note that it can cause nightmares, nausea, and other symptoms and that it may even make depression worse. Very high doses cause the body's temperature to drop, making people more likely to get viral infections. According to one doctor, "Although melatonin has many potential benefits, there is a lot of potential risk."[36] However, many people disagree with these findings. Studies done by other groups have shown positive results, with few side effects. Millions of people have been taking the supplements since the 1960s.

In addition to supplements, melatonin can be taken in the form of fish oil or by eating several servings of fish per week. Exercise, if not done in the evening, also increases melatonin levels.

Mind-body medicine

An area of increasing interest to young people is mind-body medicine. Unlike traditional Western medicine, it is based on the belief that the body and mind cannot be treated separately. This holistic view—that the body and mind are one—has been popular in the East for hundreds of years.

Mind-body medicine is a group of approaches to health that recognize a strong connection between the body and mind. For many centuries, Western medicine has treated diseases of the body and the mind separately. However, in recent years doctors and researchers have been recognizing the powerful effect the mind has on the body. Many American doctors are adding mind-body techniques to their practices.

Mind-body techniques include biofeedback, meditation, guided imagery, and hypnotherapy. They are all ways of relaxing the mind and body to focus on their natural healing processes. While they are just beginning to receive serious attention, they offer promise in treating a wide variety of disorders, including depression.

A doctor and professor of medicine who uses mind-body techniques says, "The mind/body relationship is a fascinating marriage between what people say, think, and feel, and their physiological processes. The mind moderates what goes on in the body."[37]

Biofeedback

Also known as neurotherapy, biofeedback is a treatment that uses the body's own signals to improve health.

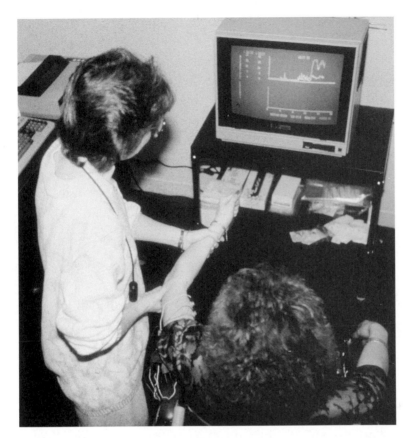

A patient receives biofeedback, or neurotherapy. The treatment helps patients exert some control over stress and the symptoms it causes.

It attempts to change the patterns of brain waves through training. The technique helps people exercise control over parts of the nervous system that regulate such functions as blood flow, skin temperature, and heart rate. As a treatment for depression, it tries to bring about the same chemical changes as antidepressants, without the side effects.

In biofeedback, parts of the body are attached with wires to a computer that measures internal activity through the skin. It senses changes in heart rate, blood pressure, muscle tension, and brain waves. As the body's tension decreases, the design that appears on the computer screen grows smaller. This teaches the patient to recognize when the mind is relaxed. Through practice, people can learn to control this relaxation response to control stress and the symptoms it causes.

Biofeedback has been used to control heart rate, blood pressure, and pain, and more recently has been applied to the treatment of depression, anxiety, sleeplessness, and alcohol and drug abuse. Its main advantage is that it lets the patient take control. As one researcher notes, "The patient is no longer the object of treatment, he *is* the treatment."[38]

Developed in the 1970s, biofeedback is one of the more widely accepted mind-body techniques among the medical community. It is practiced by many therapists licensed by the Biofeedback Certification Institute of America, and many insurance policies cover its use for a number of medical conditions.

Biofeedback is a safe technique that can be used along with other forms of therapy. Its signals may help a therapist plan and guide a patient's course of treatment. While there is little scientific evidence of its success in treating depression, it seems to help people relax and to relieve some of their symptoms.

Meditation

Meditation is a relaxation technique that reduces stress and focuses concentration. There are many forms of meditation, several of which come from Eastern traditions, such as transcendental meditation, Zen, and yoga. Newer methods include autogenic training and progressive relaxation.

All forms of meditation include the repetition of a sound, word, phrase, prayer, or muscle movement to reach a relaxed state. The person meditating returns to the repeated sound or movement whenever distracting thoughts get in the way of focusing on the present moment.

During meditation, the body's rate of energy drops, and breathing and brain-wave patterns slow down. This relaxed state helps heal stress-related disorders and relieve anxiety, anger, and depression. The benefits of meditation are recognized by many doctors, who often recommend it as part of a patient's treatment. It is a simple, safe way for people to gain control of their health.

The director of a stress reduction clinic who uses the technique says, "Meditation is a way of looking deeply into the chatter of the mind and body and becoming more aware of its patterns. By observing it, you free yourself from much of it. And then the chatter will calm down."[39]

Guided imagery

Guided imagery uses positive sensory images to bring forth the same reaction as positive experiences. These images can involve all the senses—sight, sound, smell, taste, and touch.

Doctors sometimes recommend meditation as part of their patients' treatment programs. Meditation is a safe method of reducing stress and may relieve some symptoms of depression.

People who practice this technique see depression as blocked energy and use imagery to release it. They try to create a relaxed state to help people overcome the isolation and hopeless feelings of depression.

The therapist treating depression often suggests a powerful image of a mystical cone of light. Patients are told to imagine a safe, comfortable place with the light softly descending, forming a tent of vibrant energy that surrounds and protects them. They then envision this energy entering their bodies to warm and heal them. They are encouraged to see the fog of their depression burning away as they breathe out their pain and tiredness and release their sadness.

Some psychotherapists use guided imagery as part of their treatment for depression.

Hypnotherapy

People have misleading ideas about hypnosis that were created by old movies. The image of a mysterious hypnotist swinging a pocket watch to put someone into a trance is a myth.

Hypnotherapy is a form of intense concentration that allows a person to relax and learn to control the body's functions. It is controlled by the patient, not by a hypnotist, and the person is fully conscious during the hypnotic state. People can leave this state whenever they choose to. Though its exact nature is not understood, the hypnotic state causes a change in brain-wave patterns.

A doctor who uses hypnotherapy in her practice says, "All hypnosis is self-hypnosis. It is a strategy to focus and concentrate for the purpose of achieving something that is in one's best interest." [40]

While people can practice hypnosis safely on their own, it works best if they first get instruction from a trained hypnotherapist. A hypnotherapist can teach the person to use imagery during hypnosis to change negative feelings and behavior.

Hypnotherapy is often used to treat anxiety, eating disorders, and addictions. Many people find that it works well when used along with biofeedback.

Deciding whether to try alternative therapies

Because alternative treatments are just beginning to receive serious attention by Western doctors and researchers, few long-term studies have been done to prove their effectiveness in treating depression or other mood disorders. In the decades to come, some of these treatments will probably become part of accepted Western medicine, while others will have failed the tests of modern science. Until then, most members of the psychiatric and medical professions advise caution in using them to treat serious illnesses like major depression and recommend against their use for bipolar disorder. However, they may be worth trying for milder forms of depression, such as depressive reaction or dysthymia, which often go untreated. Depressed teens who resist traditional therapies may find relief for some of their symptoms in alternative medicine.

Notes

Chapter 1: Defining Depression

1. Quoted in Kathy Cronkite, *On the Edge of Darkness: Conversations About Conquering Depression.* New York: Doubleday, 1994, p. 186.

2. Quoted in Colette Dowling, *You Mean I Don't Have to Feel This Way? New Help for Depression, Anxiety, and Addiction.* New York: Charles Scribner's Sons, 1991, p. 138.

3. Susan Dime-Meenan, "My Journey Back to Sanity," *McCall's,* October 1994, Internet Mental Health, Stories of Recovery. Available from www.mentalhealth.com/story/p52-bi01.html.

4. Cronkite, *On the Edge of Darkness,* p. 83.

5. Cronkite, *On the Edge of Darkness,* p. 80.

6. Quoted in Cronkite, *On the Edge of Darkness,* p. 20.

7. *The Journals of Sylvia Plath.* New York: Dial Press, 1982, p. 24.

Chapter 2: The Debate over Causes

8. Quoted in Peter D. Kramer, *Listening to Prozac: A Psychiatrist Explores Antidepressant Drugs and the Remaking of the Self.* New York: Viking, 1993, p. 151.

9. Quoted in Kramer, *Listening to Prozac,* p. 153.

10. Christine Gorman, "Anatomy of Melancholy: Scientists Take Pictures of Depression and Discover that It Actually Changes the Shape of the Brain," *Time,* vol. 149, no. 18, May 5, 1997, p. 78.

11. Gorman, "Anatomy of Melancholy," p. 78.

12. Quoted in Kramer, *Listening to Prozac,* p. 160.

13. Teresa Moore, "Study Reveals Deep Scars of Divorce," *San Francisco Chronicle,* June 3, 1997.

14. Deborah M. Deren, "Wings of Madness: My Experience with Clinical Depression," Internet Mental Health, May 25, 1997. Available from www.mentalhealth.com/story.

15. Pauline Anderson, "Depression Rx for Teens No Longer 'Hit or Miss'?" *Medical Post,* February 20, 1996, Internet Mental Health, Major Depressive Disorder. Available from www.mentalhealth.com/mag1/p5m-dp02.html.

16. Quoted in Cronkite, *On the Edge of Darkness,* p. 17.

17. Anderson, "Depression Rx for Teens No Longer 'Hit or Miss'?"

Chapter 3: Special Problems of Depression in Teens

18. Deren, "Wings of Madness."

19. "Mark's Story," *MDA Newsletter,* vol. 6, September/October 1995, Internet Mental Health, Stories of Recovery. Available from www.mentalhealth.com/story/p52-mark.html.

20. Dowling, *You Mean I Don't Have to Feel This Way?* pp. 106–107.

21. Denise Mann, "Unexplained Scars May Be Symptoms of 'Cutting,'" *Medical Tribune,* April 3, 1997. Available from www.medtrib.com/issues/april3/mutilation.htm.

22. Irma and Arthur Myers, *When You Feel Down—What You Can Do About It.* New York: Charles Scribner's Sons, 1982, p. 89.

23. "Student Suicides Stun Michigan School," Associated Press, *Philadelphia Daily News,* October 22, 1997.

24. Quoted in Brent Q. Hafen and Kathryn J. Frandsen, *Youth Suicide: Depression and Loneliness.* Provo, UT: Behavioral Health Associates, 1986, p. 48.

25. Mark Sauer, "Adding Up a Scenario for Disaster," *San Diego Union-Tribune,* November 6, 1997.

26. Susanna Kaysen, *Girl, Interrupted.* New York: Vintage Books, 1994, p. 37.

Chapter 4: Treating Depression

27. Quoted in Jack M. Gorman, *The New Psychiatry: The Essential Guide to State-of-the-Art Therapy, Medication, Emotional Health.* New York: St. Martin's Press, 1996, p. 58.

28. Dime-Meenan, "My Journey Back to Sanity."

29. Quoted in Michael J. Norden, *Beyond Prozac: Brain-Toxic Lifestyles, Natural Antidotes and New Generation Antidepressants.* New York: HarperCollins, 1995, p. 139.

30. Deren, "Wings of Madness."

31. Wynn Anne Sibbold, "A Haze Has Lifted to Reveal a New Day," *Medical Post,* November 7, 1995, Internet Mental Health, Major Depressive Disorder. Available from www.mentalhealth.com/story/p52-mair-html.

Chapter 5: Alternative Treatments

32. Quoted in Brigid Schulte, "Acupuncture Is Effective, Panel Finds," *San Diego Union-Tribune,* November 6, 1997.

33. Quoted in Bill Moyers, *Healing and the Mind.* New York: Doubleday, 1993, p. 268.

34. Quoted in Moyers, *Healing and the Mind,* p. 296.

35. Norden, *Beyond Prozac,* p. 35.

36. Damaris Christensen, "Melatonin Use Strongly Discouraged," New York Times Syndicate, Medical Tribune News Service, August 14, 1997. Available from nytsyn.com/live/Depression/222_081496_200130_2090.html.

37. Quoted in Moyers, *Healing and the Mind,* p. 7.

38. Quoted in Barbara B. Brown, *Stress and the Art of Biofeedback.* New York: Harper & Row, 1977, p. 2.

39. Quoted in Moyers, *Healing and the Mind,* p. 126.

40. Quoted in Moyers, *Healing and the Mind,* p. 74.

Organizations to Contact

Alcoholics Anonymous World Services
475 Riverside Dr.
New York, NY 10163
(212) 870-3400
fax: (212) 870-3003

This worldwide organization was established in 1939 to help alcoholics achieve sobriety and stay sober. The only requirement for membership is a desire to stop drinking. Alcoholics Anonymous charges no dues or fees for its meetings and is self-supporting through contributions. Its 12-step approach has formed the basis for recovery programs for many types of addiction. People can write to the above address for a list of the nearest meeting locations.

American Psychological Association
1200 17th St. NW
Washington, DC 20036
(202) 833-7600

This professional organization for psychologists aims to "advance psychology as a science, as a profession, and as a means of promoting human welfare." The APA is a source of information and educational materials on psychological research.

Narcotics Anonymous
World Services Office
PO Box 9999
Van Nuys, CA 91409
(818) 773-9999

This international community-based organization is one of the world's oldest and largest associations of recovering drug addicts. It is a nonprofit, voluntary society open to all people with any type of drug problem. The core of the program is a series of personal activities known as the Twelve Steps, adapted from Alcoholics Anonymous, and the primary service provided is the NA group meetings.

National Alliance for the Mentally Ill
200 North Glebe Rd., Suite 1015
Arlington, VA 22203-3754
(800) 950-NAMI [6264]

This nonprofit self-help organization, dedicated to helping people with mental illness and their families and friends, has over 1,200 affiliates across the United States with more than 160,000 members. It provides education about severe brain disorders, supports increased funding for research, and advocates adequate health insurance, housing, rehabilitation, and jobs for people with psychiatric illnesses. It maintains a twenty-four-hour, seven-day-a-week message line.

National Depression and Manic-Depressive Association
730 North Franklin, Suite 501
Chicago, IL 60610
(800) 826-3632

This support group for people with depression and bipolar disorder has more than 250 affiliates nationwide. Its mission is to educate patients, families, professionals, and the public concerning the nature of depressive and manic-depressive illnesses as treatable diseases; to foster self-help for patients and families; to eliminate discrimination and stigma; to improve access to care; and to advocate for research toward the elimination of these illnesses.

National Foundation for Depressive Illness
PO Box 2257
New York, NY 10116-2257
(800) 248-4344

This nonprofit organization provides telephone referrals to appropriate doctors as well as supportive literature on depression. Its 800 number offers information on services and publications, including an outreach packet for adolescents.

Suggestions for Further Reading

Mitch Golant and Susan K. Golant, *What to Do When Some-one You Love Is Depressed.* New York: Villard, 1996. A practical guide for family and friends of depressed people, designed to help them understand the disease and relate to those who suffer from it.

Lee Gutkind, *Stuck in Time: The Tragedy of Childhood Mental Illness.* New York: Henry Holt, 1993. This book documents the lives of three adolescents with mental ill-ness, including their experiences in psychiatric institutions, shelters, and group homes.

Susanna Kaysen, *Girl, Interrupted.* New York: Vintage Books, 1994. This memoir, written in diary form, covers the author's two years as an inpatient at a psychiatric institute following a suicide attempt during her late teens.

Demetri F. Papolos and Janice Papolos, *Overcoming Depression: The Definitive Resource for Patients and Families Who Live with Depression and Manic-Depression,* 3rd ed. New York: HarperCollins, 1997. This book provides current medical information and practical advice for people with depression and their families. Its focus is helping people actively participate in their own diagnosis and treatment.

Sylvia Plath, *The Bell Jar.* New York: Harper & Row, 1971. Though written as a novel, this book is based on the author's own experience with major depression as a young woman. Plath, an award-winning poet, committed suicide in her thirties.

Terrence Real, *I Don't Want to Talk About It: Overcoming the Legacy of Male Depression.* New York: Scribner, 1997. Based on the author's twenty years' experience treating men for depression, this book discusses how men consider the disease "unmanly" and try to hide it from their families, friends, and even themselves, often escaping through alcohol or abusive rage.

Works Consulted

Pauline Anderson, "Depression Rx for Teens No Longer 'Hit or Miss'?" *Medical Post,* February 20, 1996, Internet Mental Health, Major Depressive Disorder. Available from www.mentalhealth.com/mag1/p5m-dp02.html.

Maurice Blackman, "You Asked About . . . Adolescent Depression," *Canadian Journal of CME,* May 1995.

Harold H. Bloomfield, Mikael Nordfors, and Peter Williams, *Hypericum and Depression.* Los Angeles: Prelude Press, 1996.

Barbara B. Brown, *Stress and the Art of Biofeedback.* New York: Harper & Row, 1977.

Damaris Christensen, "Melatonin Use Strongly Discouraged," New York Times Syndicate, Medical Tribune News Service, August 14, 1997. Available from nytsyn.com /live/Depression/222_081496_200130_2090.html.

Kathy Cronkite, *On the Edge of Darkness: Conversations About Conquering Depression.* New York: Doubleday, 1994.

Deborah M. Deren, "Wings of Madness: My Experience with Clinical Depression," Internet Mental Health, May 25, 1997. Available from www.mentalhealth.com/story.

Susan Dime-Meenan, "My Journey Back to Sanity," *McCall's,* October 1994, Internet Mental Health, Stories of Recovery. Available from www.mentalhealth.com/story/p52-bi01.html.

Colette Dowling, *You Mean I Don't Have to Feel This Way? New Help for Depression, Anxiety, and Addiction.* New York: Charles Scribner's Sons, 1991.

"Dysthymia and Other Mood Disorders," *Harvard Mental Health Letter,* May 1991.

Jack Engler and Daniel Goleman, *The Consumer's Guide to Psychotherapy.* New York: Simon & Schuster, 1992.

Tim Friend, "Surge in Teen Drug Use, Survey Finds," *Seattle Times,* August 20, 1996.

Daniel Goleman and Joel Gurin, eds., *Mind/Body Medicine: How to Use Your Mind for Better Health.* Yonkers, NY: Consumer Reports Books, 1993.

Christine Gorman, "Anatomy of Melancholy: Scientists Take Pictures of Depression and Discover That It Actually Changes the Shape of the Brain," *Time,* vol. 149, no. 18, May 5, 1997.

Jack M. Gorman, *The New Psychiatry: The Essential Guide to State-of-the-Art Therapy, Medication, Emotional Health.* New York: St. Martin's Press, 1996.

Brent Q. Hafen and Kathryn J. Frandsen, *Youth Suicide: Depression and Loneliness.* Provo, UT: Behavioral Health Associates, 1986.

"Heredity vs. Environment in Depression," *Harvard Mental Health Letter,* July 1995.

"Interpersonal Aspects of Depression," *Harvard Mental Health Letter,* October 1989.

The Journals of Sylvia Plath. New York: Dial Press, 1982.

Donald F. Klein and Paul H. Wender, *Understanding Depression: A Complete Guide to Diagnosis and Treatment.* New York: Oxford University Press, 1993.

Peter D. Kramer, *Listening to Prozac: A Psychiatrist Explores Antidepressant Drugs and the Remaking of the Self.* New York: Viking, 1993.

Denise Mann, "Unexplained Scars May Be Symptoms of 'Cutting,'" *Medical Tribune,* April 3, 1997. Available from www.medtrib.com/issues/april3/mutilation.htm.

"Mark's Story," *MDA Newsletter,* vol. 6, September/October 1995, Internet Mental Health, Stories of Recovery. Available from www.mentalhealth.com/story/p52-mark.html.

Francis Mark Mondimore, *Depression: The Mood Disease,* rev. ed. Baltimore: Johns Hopkins University Press, 1993.

Teresa Moore, "Study Reveals Deep Scars of Divorce," *San Francisco Chronicle,* June 3, 1997.

Bill Moyers, *Healing and the Mind.* New York: Doubleday, 1993.

Irma and Arthur Myers, *When You Feel Down—What You Can Do About It.* New York: Charles Scribner's Sons, 1982.

"Nature vs. Nurture," *Online NewsHour,* PBS broadcast, May 14, 1996 (David Gergen interview with Winifred Gallagher, author of *I.D.: How Heredity and Experience Make You What You Are).*

Michael J. Norden, *Beyond Prozac: Brain-Toxic Lifestyles, Natural Antidotes and New Generation Antidepressants.* New York: HarperCollins, 1995.

Mike Robinson, "Prozac Effective in Fighting Depression in Young People," Associated Press, November 14, 1997. Available from search.nando.net/plweb.cgi/fastweb.

Mark Sauer, "Adding Up a Scenario for Disaster," *San Diego Union-Tribune,* November 6, 1997.

Brigid Schulte, "Acupuncture Is Effective, Panel Finds," *San Diego Union-Tribune,* November 6, 1997.

Wynn Anne Sibbold, "A Haze Has Lifted to Reveal a New Day," *Medical Post,* November 7, 1995, Internet Mental Health, Major Depressive Disorder. Available from www. mentalhealth.com/story/p52-mair-html.

Robert Somerville, project ed., *The Medical Advisor: The Complete Guide to Alternative and Conventional Treatments.* New York: Time-Life Books, 1997.

"Student Suicides Stun Michigan School," Associated Press, *Philadelphia Daily News,* October 22, 1997.

Julian Whitaker, *Dr. Whitaker's Guide to Natural Healing.* Rocklin, CA: Prima Publishing, 1995.

Index

Picture Credits

Cover photo: © David Young Wolff/Tony Stone Images, Inc.
AP/Wide World Photos, 28
© Bruce Ayres/Tony Stone Images, Inc., 44
© Richard Bermack/Impact Visuals, 51
© Nina Berman/Sipa Press, 43
© Donna Binder/Impact Visuals, 47
© Jon Bradley/Tony Stone Images, Inc., 58
Don Hogan Charles/New York Times Company/Archive
     Photos, 22
© Condyles/Impact Visuals, 38
© Kate Connell/Tony Stone Images, Inc., 34
© Robert E. Daemmrich/Tony Stone Images, Inc., 64, 82
© Bob Daemmrich/Uniphoto, 49
© Florence Durand/Sipa Press, 69
© Amy C. Elliott/Ace Photography, 12
© Harvey Finkle/Custom Medical Stock Photo, 89
© Hazel Hankin/Impact Visuals, 7
© Zigy Kaluzny/Tony Stone Images, Inc., 60
© F. M. Kearney/Impact Visuals, 78
Library of Congress, 25, 28
© Andrew Lichtenstein/Impact Visuals, 41
© Will & Deni McIntyre/Tony Stone Images, Inc., 86
National Archives, 21 (both)
© Rosanne Olson/Tony Stone Images, Inc., 74
© Gretchen Palmer/Uniphoto, 91
© Frank Siteman/Tony Stone Images, Inc., 19
© Martha Tabor/Impact Visuals, 79
© Jim West/Impact Visuals, 33
© David Young Wolff/Tony Stone Images, Inc., 85

About the Author

Lisa Wolff is a writer and editor with many years of staff experience at New York publishing houses. She currently lives in San Diego, where she edits reference books and writes articles on health and fitness.